INDULGE

ROWIE DILLON

HarperCollins*Publishers*

for Lynnie

I wish you were here to see and read this

Contents

BREAKFAST 11
BRUNCH, LUNCH AND SALADY BITS 27
DINNER 47
PASTRY, PIES, PIZZA AND PASTA 71
BIG CAKES, LITTLE CAKES 101
THE SWEETEST THINGS 125
BIKKIES, SLICES AND SNACKS 147
THE ENTERTAINER 175
PARTY, PARTY, PARTY! 189
THE SCIENCE OF FLOURS 209
INDEX 219

INTRODUCTION

Welcome to my journey, my passion and my dream. I've had a lifelong love affair with food and entertaining, I love cooking and creating a juxtaposition of flavours that deliver the best possible taste. In a nutshell, I find cooking cathartic.

At my 40th birthday party, I asked my three sisters to say something. In succession from youngest to oldest they all spoke. It was when my baby sister, Simone, spoke that that the penny dropped. Sim said, 'My sister Rowena is very creative, to the point where she doesn't even realise it. It's natural to her, she thinks it's how we all think. How anyone can create a gourmet meal from an empty pantry is beyond me, but Rowie does it without a care in the world and delivers you something that looks and tastes sensational.' I couldn't believe her words – it was the biggest compliment that I have ever had. Bless you, Sim.

Ten years ago, I was given the task of making Christmas dessert. I opted to pass on the pud and this led to the creation of Rowie's Rich Orange and Almond Cake, free of wheat, yeast, dairy and gluten. From this my beautiful business, Rowie's Cakes: a kitchen that bakes wheat, yeast, dairy and gluten free, was born.

It's grown from a small business of a couple of people to a business that employs 20 people and produces thousands of cakes a day; we carve up reams of rocky road by the pallet, and ship handmade cakes, bikkies and desserts to ports all around the country and, more recently, overseas.

I am passionate about my business and my brand and the main reason for its success is the fact that I am one determined woman on a mission: to make it possible for allergy sufferers to enjoy indulgent, great-tasting food.

Being told you're gluten intolerant or coeliac is heartbreaking for some, but believe me, there is no reason to feel like you've been relegated to a life of culinary boredom. I am gluten intolerant and the food I eat is anything but boring.

Cook your way through this collection and give your family, friends and guests (with allergies or not) the proof that it is possible to create indulgent, simple and yummy gluten-free food that is not boring or bland. Experiment, be creative and feel comfortable about indulging in the food you thought you could never serve or eat again. Look at the ingredients in your pantry and make them your friends.

Give yourself the time to shop for ingredients, relax into cooking and then you can eliminate bland cuisine from your life – forever.

In the Science of Flours chapter, discover the texture of different grains and how this knowledge is used in their application. Learn how you can create texture, flavour, and bounce and elasticity from the properties of the grain. Embrace experimental baking and be willing to try the flours used here to create pies, cakes, pastries, tarts and breads from scratch.

I hope *Indulge* will inspire you and make you happy and you might enjoy the story it tells along the way. I love what I do and I hope you will too. Happy cooking and may you find my collection of recipes and ideas enticing, inviting and life changing!

Enjoy and Indulge!

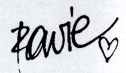

IMPORTANT INFORMATION

All care has been taken in the compiling of the contents, but this book does not take account of individual circumstances, individual dietary intolerances, allergies and nutritional needs. The author and publisher cannot be held responsible for any claim or action that may arise from reliance on the information contained in this book. Before embarking on a gluten-free diet it is important that you obtain the advice of a medical practitioner, health-care professional or accredited practicing dietician.

When purchasing products listed as ingredients in this book, always read the labels carefully to ensure they are gluten-free.

Breakfast

A week's worth of breakfast.
Warm, hot or cold, these recipes will leave
you well prepared for the day ahead.

BERRY AND CHOCOLATE BUCKWHEAT HOTCAKES

Makes 10

For those of us who suffer from gluten intolerance, the quest for sustenance at breakfast is eternal. These hotcakes warm my tum and keep me content all day – plus they are not too sugary. Yum, yum!

340g (1⅓ cups) ricotta

185ml (¾ cup) milk

4 eggs, separated

130g (1 cup) buckwheat flour

1 teaspoon gluten-free baking powder

1 tablespoon gluten-free cocoa powder

pinch of salt

50–75g unsalted butter, softened, for greasing

200g mixed berries

pure icing sugar, sifted, for dusting

warmed honey or maple syrup, for drizzling

Place the ricotta, milk and egg yolks in a bowl and stir to combine.

Sift the flour, baking powder, cocoa and salt into the ricotta mixture and stir until well combined.

Beat the egg whites in a large bowl until stiff peaks form. Fold the egg whites into the ricotta mixture in two or three batches.

Lightly grease a large non-stick frying pan with one-third of the butter until foaming. Drop 2 tablespoons of batter per hotcake into the pan and cook, covered, in batches of three over medium heat for 2 minutes until the hotcakes are golden on the underside. Turn the hotcakes and cook on the other side until golden brown and cooked through. Transfer to a plate and keep warm. Repeat with remaining butter and batter to make 10 hotcakes.

Layer two or three hotcakes with mixed berries on each serving plate. Dust with the icing sugar, drizzle with the honey or maple syrup and serve.

COCONUT AND CINNAMON BREAD

Makes 8–10 slices

Absolutely beautiful toasted or grilled.

2 eggs
300ml milk
½ teaspoon vanilla extract
260g (2 cups) quinoa flour
2 teaspoons gluten-free baking powder
2 teaspoons ground cinnamon
230g (1 cup) caster sugar
150g (1¾ cups) desiccated coconut
75g unsalted butter, melted
pure icing sugar, sifted, for dusting

Preheat the oven to 180°C. Grease and line a 20cm loaf tin.

Whisk the eggs, milk and vanilla in a small bowl. Sift the flour, baking powder and cinnamon into a separate bowl. Add the caster sugar and coconut and stir to combine.

Gradually add the egg mixture to the dry mixture and stir until combined, then mix in the melted butter. Pour into the prepared loaf tin and bake for 50 minutes, or until a skewer inserted into the middle comes out clean. Set aside to cool in the tin on a wire rack. Remove from the tin, cut into thick slices and dust with the icing sugar.

RICE PUDDING WITH POACHED STONE FRUIT

Serves 6

This lovely pudding will warm you from head to toe. It reminds me of cold mornings in slippers and a dressing gown preparing for a winter's day.

RICE PUDDING

1 litre water

300g (1½ cups) short-grain white rice

750ml (3 cups) hot milk

250ml (1 cup) hot cream

170g (¾ cup) caster sugar, plus 90g extra, for dusting

20g unsalted butter

3 egg yolks

½ teaspoon ground cinnamon

½ teaspoon vanilla extract

poached stone fruit (see recipe over page)

Bring the water to the boil in a large saucepan. Add the rice and cook, stirring occasionally, over low heat for 10–15 minutes, or until the water is absorbed.

Add 250ml (1 cup) of the hot milk and cook, stirring occasionally, for 3–5 minutes. Add the remaining milk, 125ml (½ cup) at a time, and stir until all the milk is absorbed. Stir in the hot cream, sugar, butter, egg yolks, cinnamon and vanilla and cook for a further 10 minutes until the mixture is very creamy.

Spoon into a 2 litre (8 cup) capacity flameproof baking dish, cool, cover with plastic wrap and refrigerate until cold. The pudding will keep in the refrigerator for up to 3 days before use.

Sprinkle the extra sugar over the pudding and place under a hot grill until caramelised.

To serve, spoon one ladle (½ cup) of the warmed pudding into a bowl, then top with 1 tablespoon of the poached stone fruit and 2 tablespoons of the sugar syrup.

 *continued*

RICE PUDDING WITH POACHED STONE FRUIT

continued

POACHED STONE FRUIT

1kg mixed peaches, nectarines, apricots and plums

1 orange

140g (¾ cup, lightly packed) brown sugar

1 vanilla bean, split in half lengthways

2 cinnamon sticks

500ml (2 cups) water

Plunge the peaches, nectarines, apricots and plums, in batches, into a large saucepan of boiling water for 1 minute. Remove with a slotted spoon, set aside until cool enough to handle, then peel.

Halve and stone the peaches, nectarines, apricots and plums.

Using a vegetable peeler, peel the zest from the orange, then, using a small, sharp knife remove any white pith. Juice the orange.

Combine the orange zest and juice with the sugar, vanilla bean, cinnamon sticks and water in a saucepan large enough to hold all the fruit and stir over medium heat until the sugar dissolves. Bring to a simmer, add all the fruit and gently poach for 5–8 minutes, or until just tender.

Serve warm, or allow to cool in the syrup and serve at room temperature. The poached stone fruit will keep, covered, in the refrigerator for up to 3 days.

HOT AND COLD FRUIT SALAD

Serves 4

Add a little theatre to breakfast with the delicious and dramatic contrast of hot and cold fruit.

4 peaches

110g (1¼ cups) flaked almonds

140g pure icing sugar

½ rockmelon or green melon

4 mango cheeks

250g strawberries, hulled

250g green and red seedless grapes

Halve the peaches and remove the stones. Place cut-side up on a baking tray and sprinkle on the almonds. Sift the icing sugar over the top and place under a hot grill for 5 minutes, or until the peaches and almonds begin to brown and the sugar caramelises.

Meanwhile, cut the melon and mango into the desired shapes (I used a heart-shaped cutter) and chop the strawberries into nice big pieces.

Quickly cook the melon and mango shapes in a very hot chargrill pan for 1–2 minutes on each side, then set aside.

Place the strawberries and grapes in a large serving bowl. Add the warmed fruit and the almonds and, using your hands, gently toss. Divide the mixture between four bowls and serve immediately.

Create hearts, stars, bells, circles or diamonds with your chargrilled fruit — it just depends what your theme is. If it's someone's birthday, you might like to use numbers.

TOASTED MUESLI

Makes a week's worth of brekkie

Once you get into the swing of spending ten minutes on a Sunday to prepare breakfast for the week ahead, you'll be hooked by how easy and efficient muesli-making can be. What a lovely way to start the day!

225g (3½ cups) golden rice flakes

3 tablespoons pepitas

3 tablespoons sunflower seeds

75g (3 cups) puffed amaranth

3 teaspoons golden linseeds

3 tablespoons dried diced pineapple

3 tablespoons finely sliced dried mango

3 tablespoons sultanas or raisins

3 tablespoons pitted chopped or torn dates

natural yoghurt, fresh fruit and honey, to serve

Line a baking tray with baking paper. Sprinkle 1 cup of the rice flakes onto the prepared tray. Scatter the pepitas and sunflower seeds over the rice flakes and place under a warm grill for 5 minutes, or until the rice flakes and seeds begin to brown.

Mix together all the remaining ingredients in a large bowl. Add the toasted ingredients, mix well and transfer to an airtight container for up to 2 weeks. Serve with yoghurt, fresh fruit and a drizzle of honey.

CHIA BREAD

Makes 1 loaf

For brekkie on the hop, this tasty bread is incredibly easy to make – in three steps and in under five minutes you will have it in the oven. Indulging in freshly baked bread first thing in the morning – I can't imagine a more satisfying start to the day.

1 tablespoon chia seeds

350g (2 cups) rice flour

3 tablespoons caster sugar

3 teaspoons gluten-free baking powder

2 eggs, beaten

250ml (1 cup) milk

60ml (¼ cup) vegetable oil

Preheat the oven to 180°C. Line a 20cm loaf tin with baking paper.

Soak the chia seeds in 125ml (½ cup) water for 3–5 minutes. Place all the dry ingredients in a large bowl and stir to combine. Make a well in the centre and stir in the beaten eggs. Add the milk and oil, stirring as you add each ingredient, ensuring the batter doesn't go lumpy. Stir to combine, then drain and add the chia seeds.

Pour into the prepared loaf tin and bake on the centre shelf of the oven for 30–35 minutes, or until golden on top and when a skewer inserted into the middle comes out clean.

Brunch, lunch and salady bits

Mix and match salads with a light lunch of frittata or burgerettes; try sushi for nibbles; or pile a plate with a combination of salads and let those crunchy, sweet and spicy flavours tempt your tastebuds. These recipes are easy to make and can be prepared ahead, which should give you some time back, away from the kitchen, to put your feet up and enjoy.

SUSHI SANDWICHES

Serves 4

This is a gorgeous take on a universal favourite and an ideal choice for an afternoon tea celebration partnered with some little cakes or pastries and a cup of herbal tea. I once made these for a friend's baby shower and stacked them on top of a beautiful glass cake stand for that extra touch of glamour.

465g (2½ cups) cooked short-grain white rice, cooled

2 tablespoons water

2 tablespoons rice wine vinegar

1 tablespoon caster sugar

2 sheets of nori

8 slices of thinly cut sashimi-grade salmon

1 cucumber, deseeded and sliced

Combine the cooked rice, water, vinegar and sugar in a bowl and mix well.

Spread half the rice on one nori sheet and top with the salmon and cucumber. Spread the rest of the rice over the remaining nori sheet and flip on top of the filling. Press down firmly and carefully cut the sushi sandwich into small squares using a sharp knife.

If you are worried about cutting the sushi sandwich because it's too delicate, place it in the freezer on a lined tray for 30 minutes, then try cutting gently with a sharp knife.

FRIENDLY FRITTATA

Serves 8

I call this frittata 'friendly' because it's an all-round crowd pleaser; perfect for a light lunch with a few friends or an easy way to feed a whole lot of friends at a swim-over on a hot summer's day. Add a crisp salad and a dollop of chutney and it will be devoured in no time. Try my slightly different take on chutney on page 169.

8 eggs, beaten

125ml (½ cup) thickened cream

50g (½ cup) grated Parmesan

2 spring onions, chopped

60g baby English spinach leaves

a small handful of mixed herbs, such as parsley, chervil and basil

150g smoked salmon, roughly torn

60g crumbled feta

Preheat the oven to 180°C. Grease and line a 21cm round pie dish.

Combine the eggs, cream, Parmesan, spring onion, spinach, herbs and salmon in a bowl and lightly beat. Pour the mixture into the pie dish, crumble the feta on top and season with salt and pepper.

Bake for 25 minutes, or until firm to touch in the centre.

SAFFRON RICE WITH PISTACHIO AND RADISH

Serves 4

A simple yet exotic rice salad that makes a colourful addition to any meal, or gorgeous served on its own with some crunchy leafy greens.

250ml (1 cup) gluten-free chicken stock

250ml (1 cup) water

pinch of saffron threads

40g unsalted butter

1 large brown onion, finely chopped

200g (1 cup) long-grain white rice

65g (½ cup) smashed pistachio nuts

3 radishes, thinly sliced

Combine the stock and water in a saucepan over medium heat and bring to the boil. Add the saffron and remove from the heat.

Melt the butter in another saucepan over medium heat, add the onion and cook, stirring occasionally, until golden brown. Stir in the rice until coated with the onion mixture and cook, stirring, for 3 minutes. Pour in the stock mixture and stir. Season with salt and pepper, cover and gently bring to the boil. Reduce the heat to low and steam for 15 minutes, or until the rice is tender and all the liquid is absorbed.

Remove from the heat and stand, covered, for 5 minutes. Stir in the smashed pistachios and sliced radish, fluffing it up with a fork, and serve.

SWEET AND SPICY COLESLAW

Serves 4

Slaw is special. The colour and robust flavours elevate this simple creation to a culinary work of art. It might be considered a little daggy; I've been waiting nearly twenty years for it to come back in fashion – and I'm still waiting! Nevertheless, I'm willing to declare my lifelong devotion to this retro gem.

250g red cabbage, finely shredded

250g green cabbage, finely shredded

2 carrots, peeled and grated

1 white onion, grated

DRESSING

60g (¼ cup) whole-egg gluten-free mayonnaise

1 tablespoon gluten-free Dijon mustard

2 teaspoons apple cider vinegar

1 tablespoon caster sugar

½ teaspoon black pepper

¼ teaspoon cayenne pepper

Combine the cabbages, carrot and onion in a large bowl.

To make the dressing, place the mayonnaise, mustard, vinegar, sugar and peppers in a bowl and whisk to combine.

Add the dressing to the slaw and toss to combine. Cover with plastic wrap and refrigerate for up to 2 hours to allow the flavours to develop. Toss and roll your slaw and serve.

PARSLEY AND QUINOA SALAD

Serves 4

Quinoa – pronounced 'keen-wah' – is a gorgeous grain packed with goodness. At Rowie's Cakes we use it in a flour form to bake cakes and bread. I love the fact that it's high in protein, fluffy and absorbent, plus it has a full-bodied, earthy taste. Here it makes for a nutty-tasting salad with a fresh and bountiful flavour.

150g (¾ cup) quinoa, rinsed (combination of red and plain quinoa)

375ml (1½ cups) water

1½ tablespoons lemon juice

1 teaspoon extra virgin olive oil

⅓ cup flat-leaf parsley, roughly chopped

1 small Lebanese cucumber, peeled, deseeded and diced

Combine the quinoa and water in a saucepan over medium–high heat, cover and bring to the boil. Reduce the heat to low and simmer for 10 minutes, or until the water is absorbed. Drain, then rinse well and transfer to a large bowl.

To make the dressing, whisk the lemon juice and olive oil in a small bowl and season with a generous amount of salt and pepper. Add the parsley, cucumber and dressing to the quinoa and toss to combine.

BABY BEET AND ORANGE SALAD

Could this dish look any more gorgeous? A spectacular salad with flavour bursts of orange, beetroot and pomegranate, it will make your cheeks rosy and lends a brilliant splash of colour to the table.

2 oranges, skin on

8–10 baby beets, skin on, leaves trimmed and stems cut about 2cm above bulb

olive oil, for drizzling

¼ cup chervil leaves

1 pomegranate, seeds only

raspberry vinegar, for drizzling

Place the whole oranges in a large saucepan, cover with water and bring to the boil for 30 minutes. Drain and set aside. (You can prepare the oranges and the beets the day before if you like, but don't peel them until ready for use the next day).

Wash the beets, being careful not to break the skin, and place in a large saucepan, cover with water and bring to the boil. Reduce to a simmer for 30 minutes, or until beets are tender when tested with a skewer. Drain and set aside.

Peel the oranges using a sharp knife, then cut into slices, crossways, delicately removing any seeds. Peel the beets carefully (I use gloves so my hands don't stain). Arrange the orange and beets on a serving platter and drizzle with the olive oil.

Combine the chervil and pomegranate seeds in a bowl, then scatter over the assembled platter. Finish with a splash of olive oil and raspberry vinegar and season with cracked black pepper.

CHICKEN SANDWICHES

Makes 6 regular or 12 mini

Ah, the humble sandwich – so versatile and classic. Some gluten-free bread can be best described as having a rock-like texture: very hard and crumbles to bits. With a bit of experimentation I've come up with a bread that is light and fluffy, and doesn't crumble when cut. This is best sliced before freezing.

BREAD

Use the chia bread recipe on page 24, replacing the chia seeds with linseeds, poppy seeds or caraway seeds

FILLING

350g (2 cups) finely shredded cooked chicken

3 tablespoons mashed potato

1 tablespoon chopped flat-leaf parsley

2 celery stalks, finely chopped

1 tablespoon rice bran oil

1 Lebanese cucumber, finely diced

1 spring onion, green part only, roughly chopped

3 radishes, thinly sliced

To make the filling, combine all the filling ingredients in a large bowl.

Cut the loaf of bread into 12 slices. Spread the filling on six slices, then top each with another slice of bread. Remove the crusts and cut each sandwich in half or into shapes.

BURGERETTES

Makes 12

These give a wow to entertaining, the lunchbox or a lazy day at home spent soaking up the sun. They are also an amazing Saturday afternoon snack for a hungry tribe. For a classic meatball dish, combine the patties with an Italian-inspired tomato sauce (see page 96) and lash with basil leaves and some Pecorino or Parmesan.

BURGERETTES

300g beef or veal mince

200g mashed potato

a small handful of flat-leaf parsley, finely chopped

1 garlic clove, finely chopped

50g (⅓ cup) quinoa flour

2 tablespoons soy milk

1 egg, beaten

olive oil, for frying

TO SERVE

12 rice flour buns (see recipe over page)

3 tomatoes, sliced

6 baby cos or butter lettuce leaves, torn

Combine the mince, mashed potato, parsley and garlic in a bowl and mix well.

Soak the quinoa flour in the soy milk for 5 minutes. Pour off the excess liquid and add to the mince mixture along with the egg. Season with the salt and pepper and mix well. Cover with plastic wrap and refrigerate for 30 minutes.

Shape the mixture into 12 mini burger patties. Heat the oil in a large frying pan over medium heat, add the patties, in batches, and fry for 3–5 minutes on each side, or until golden brown and just cooked through.

Cut a rice flour bun in two. Place a patty on the bottom bun, add a slice of tomato and some lettuce and finish with the top bun. Repeat with the remaining buns and patties, tomato and lettuce.

 continued

BURGERETTES

continued

RICE FLOUR BUNS

80ml (⅓ cup) olive oil

2 eggs, at room temperature

430g (2½ cups) rice flour

40g (⅓ cup) arrowroot

40g (⅓ cup) soy flour

40g (⅓ cup) amaranth flour

1 tablespoon caster sugar

1½ teaspoons salt

1 tablespoon xanthan gum

1 x 7g sachet (1½ teaspoons) gluten-free dried yeast

400ml of warm water

50ml soda water, at room temperature

2 tablespoons sesame seeds

Grease and line a large baking tray.

Place all the ingredients in the order they appear, except the soda water and sesame seeds, in a large mixing bowl. Combine well with a wooden spoon then add the soda water and bring together with your hands to form a sticky dough. Knead well for 5 minutes. Cover bowl with plastic wrap and set aside in a warm place for 15–20 minutes. Your buns will not rise very much during this time.

Preheat the oven to 200°C. Knead again for 2 minutes, or until firm. Shape the dough into 12 small buns and place on the prepared tray. Dip your fingers in some water and gently smooth the top of the buns. Sprinkle each bun with sesame seeds and bake buns for 15 minutes, or until golden on top. Allow to cool on the tray for 3 minutes then transfer to a wire rack to cool completely.

Dinner

I may be known for my sweet treats, but I've also cooked my way through many a dinner party over the years and this is a small selection of my favourites. These are meals that everyone, gluten-intolerant or not, will enjoy. When you're planning a special dinner, add a starter, appetiser or dessert from the other chapters for a memorable menu and evening.

ROAST CHOOK WITH LEMON, THYME AND SZECHUAN SALT AND PEPPER

Serves 6

This is my favourite way to do a roast chook. The trick to this recipe is the use of an oven bag. It keeps your oven clean and delivers the most wonderful, succulent bird you have ever tasted. Use organic chicken, if you can, and if you haven't got Szechuan pepper use cracked black or pink peppercorns.

1 tablespoon ground Szechuan pepper

1 tablespoon salt

olive oil

1 x 2kg (size 20) organic chicken

2 tablespoons brown rice flour

1 lemon, zested

3 garlic cloves, halved

1 teaspoon finely chopped fresh ginger

¼ cup thyme leaves

4 preserved lemon quarters, flesh on

1 lemon, halved

Combine the Szechuan pepper and salt in a non-stick frying pan and dry fry over medium heat for 2–3 minutes, or until fragrant.

Preheat the oven to 180°C. Rub the olive oil all over the chook. Combine the Szechuan seasoning, rice flour and zest in a large oven bag and shake to coat the inside of the bag.

Place the garlic, ginger, thyme and preserved lemon inside the cavity of the chook. Squeeze the juice from the halved lemon into the cavity, then add the lemon halves and tie up the legs with kitchen twine, so all the goodies don't fall out.

Shake the bag, add the chook and seal the opening with a twist tie. Shake again to evenly coat the chook with the seasoned flour. Place in a roasting tin and roast for 1 hour, or until the juices run clear when the thigh is pierced with the tip of a sharp knife. Serve with seasonal vegetables.

CHICKEN SCHNITZEL

Serves 4

This festhaus classic is the ultimate in comfort food.
It can also be adapted for veal or fish.

130g (2 cups) golden rice flakes

90g (½ cup) rice flour

2 eggs, beaten

2 whole chicken breasts, malleted and cut into 4 even pieces

2 tablespoons rice bran oil or vegetable oil

MASH

6 garlic cloves

olive oil, for drizzling

4 (750g) desiree or sebago potatoes, peeled

100g butter

2 tablespoons milk

1 tablespoon chopped flat-leaf parsley

Preheat the oven to 180°C. Line a baking tray with baking paper.

Combine the rice flakes and rice flour in a food processor and pulse until the mixture resembles fine breadcrumbs. Transfer the mixture to a medium bowl or onto a plate.

Gently dip each chicken piece in the beaten egg mixture then coat evenly in breadcrumbs and set aside.

Heat the rice bran oil over medium–high heat in a large frying pan. Add the chicken and cook evenly for 4–5 minutes each side. (Lower the heat to medium if the schnitzels are browning too quickly on the edges.) Transfer the chicken onto paper towels to drain, then cover with foil or place in a temperate oven to keep warm.

To make the mash, place the garlic on the prepared tray and drizzle with a little olive oil. Bake for 20 minutes, or until golden brown.

Place whole potatoes in a large saucepan and cover with water. Bring to the boil and cook for 15–20 minutes. Drain and set aside.

Mash the potatoes with a fork, add the butter and milk and stir vigorously. Peel the garlic and fold through the mash with the parsley and season with salt and pepper. Serve with the schnitzel.

TURKEY BREAST WITH HERB AND ALMOND BUTTER

Serves 6

Gobble, gobble! That's what you'll be doing when you eat this dish. The orange zest infuses with the herbs and the velvet quality of the turkey breast to give you a delicious and modern take on a traditional family favourite.

125g butter, softened

2 garlic cloves, crushed

2 tablespoons chopped tarragon leaves

2 tablespoons finely chopped chives

2 tablespoons chopped flat-leaf parsley

1 tablespoon flaked almonds

1 tablespoon finely grated orange zest

1kg turkey breast fillet, skin on

2 tablespoons olive oil

Preheat the oven to 180°C.

Combine the butter, garlic, tarragon, chives, parsley, almonds and orange zest in a bowl and use your hands (in gloves if you wish) to bring the mixture together.

Place the turkey, skin-side up, on a work surface and, using your fingers, gently lift the skin away from the flesh to form a pocket. Gently and evenly stuff the herb and almond butter under the skin.

Brush the turkey with the oil and season with salt and pepper. Transfer to a wire rack in a large roasting pan, cover with foil and roast for 30 minutes. Remove the foil and roast, basting with the pan juices every 10 minutes, for a further 30 minutes, or until cooked through. Set aside to rest for 10 minutes. Slice and serve.

enjoy

APPLE, LEEK AND PUMPKIN GRATIN

Serves 6

This recipe is for my friends Melanie and Natalie. It is hard to render these girls speechless at any time, but Melanie could hardly get a word out when she tried this gratin. And they both raved about *those* vegetables for days after. The combination of apple and vegetables produces a magnificent flavour. If you're not into Parmesan, sprinkle with more sage and season with extra salt and pepper. These veggies rock!

125ml (½ cup) rice bran oil, plus 1 tablespoon extra for brushing

2 leeks, white part only, halved lengthways and thinly sliced

2 tablespoons water

250ml (1 cup) gluten-free vegetable stock

1 tablespoon chopped sage leaves

500g butternut pumpkin, cut into 5mm thick slices

450g green apples, cored and cut into 5mm thick slices

50g (½ cup) grated Parmesan

Preheat the oven to 180°C. Lightly grease a 20 x 20cm baking dish.

Heat the oil in a frying pan over medium heat. Add the leek and water, season with salt and pepper and cook for 1 minute until the leek begins to soften. Add 125ml (½ cup) of the stock and the sage and cook for 2 minutes, or until the liquid is reduced to a glaze. Set aside.

Arrange half of the pumpkin, in overlapping slices, in the prepared dish and season with salt and pepper. Spread the leek evenly over the pumpkin, then arrange the apple in a layer over the leek. Top with the remaining pumpkin and season with salt and pepper. Pour in the remaining stock and brush the pumpkin with the extra oil. Cover with foil and bake for 45 minutes. Remove from the oven and sprinkle on the Parmesan. Return, uncovered, to the oven and bake for 10 minutes, or until the Parmesan is golden brown and crisp. Set aside to cool for 3–5 minutes. Serve warm.

MUSHROOM AND BASIL STUFFED BAKED ONIONS

Serves 4

Here's a pearler for all the vegetarians out there and another wonderful way to use veggies that stands out from the crowd. It can be served as an accompaniment to Apple, leek and pumpkin gratin (see page 54) or Rolled pork belly (see page 60).

4 brown onions, unpeeled

1 garlic clove, peeled

a handful of basil leaves

a small handful of flat-leaf parsley

½ teaspoon sea salt

¼ teaspoon black pepper

250g cold mashed potato

1 tablespoon olive oil

140g Swiss brown mushrooms, peeled and thinly sliced

1 tablespoon dry white wine

Preheat the oven to 220°C.

Cut off the top quarter from each onion and individually wrap the onions in foil. Bake the onions for 1½ hours until soft. (You can do this step a day ahead to save time if you wish.) Unwrap the onions and allow to cool for 15 minutes, then peel, discarding the skin. Remove the flesh from the centre of each onion, leaving only two outer layers to form a shell. Set aside 1 cup of the cooked onion flesh and place the onion shells in a small baking dish.

Place the reserved onion flesh, garlic, basil, parsley, salt and pepper in a food processor and puree. Add the mashed potato and pulse to combine.

Heat the oil in a small frying pan over medium heat, add the mushroom and cook until lightly golden.

Stuff the onion shells with alternating spoonfuls of the potato and onion mash and the mushroom. Pour the wine into the baking dish and bake for 30 minutes, or until soft and golden. Serve warm.

BEEF WELLINGTON

Serves 6

I adore this Beef Wellington recipe. It reminds me of family dinners we used to have at the local yacht club on a Saturday night – the piano man would grab our little fingers and push them down on the keys, letting us think we were masters on the piano! Serve with some lemony green beans.

650g beef eye fillet, trimmed of fat

2 tablespoons olive oil

50g gluten-free chicken liver pâté

115g button mushrooms, thinly sliced

1 egg, lightly beaten

PASTRY

85g (⅔ cup) gluten-free cornflour

90g (½ cup) rice flour

1 teaspoon gluten-free baking powder

½ teaspoon salt

100g butter, chilled, cut into 1cm cubes

200g cold mashed potato

To make the pastry, pulse the cornflour, rice flour, baking powder and salt in a food processor to combine. Add the butter and pulse until the mixture resembles fine breadcrumbs. Then add the potato and process until the dough just comes together.

Knead the dough on a lightly floured surface until smooth. Shape into a disc, cover with plastic wrap or baking paper and set aside.

Season the beef with salt and pepper. Heat the oil in a large frying pan over high heat, add the beef and quickly brown on all sides. This will take about 6 minutes. Transfer the beef to a wire rack over a baking tray and set aside for 10 minutes, or until cool to touch.

Roll out the pastry on a lightly floured piece of baking paper to form a 20 x 30cm rectangle.

Spread the pâté over the beef and arrange the mushroom over the top and sides. Place the coated beef on the pastry and fold the pastry around the beef to enclose. Place, seam-side down, on a baking tray. Brush the pastry with the egg and place in the fridge for 20 minutes.

Preheat the oven to 180°C. Bake the beef for 35–40 minutes for medium, or until the beef is cooked to your liking. Remove from the oven and rest for 10 minutes before slicing and serving.

 This pastry is ideal for wrapping and enclosing beef, fish or even mince – it's great for pasties.

ROLLED PORK BELLY WITH PRUNES AND QUINOA

Serves 6–8

Stuffing is another one of those yummy foods that the gluten-intolerant must normally forgo, but not any longer! This fantastic stuffing is incredibly versatile – try using it in a chicken or even a Christmas turkey. The ingredients are not fixed and can be substituted to suit your taste – figs or dates instead of prunes; feel free to experiment.

3 tablespoons maple syrup

150g pitted prunes

1.6kg boneless pork belly, skin scored

STUFFING

80ml (⅓ cup) olive oil

1 onion, thinly sliced

3 garlic cloves, finely chopped

1 tablespoon raspberry vinegar

130g quinoa flakes

2 tablespoons finely chopped sage leaves

Preheat the oven to 250°C. To make the stuffing, heat the oil in a saucepan over medium–low heat. Add the onion and garlic and sauté until golden. Add the vinegar and simmer for 1–2 minutes until evaporated. Stir in the quinoa and sage and season to taste. Set aside to cool.

Pour the maple syrup into a small saucepan and bring to a simmer. Add the prunes, return to a simmer, then set aside.

Place the pork on a work surface, skin-side down, with one long side facing you. Season with salt and pepper and spread with an even layer of stuffing. Arrange the poached prunes in a line in the centre and roll up the pork to enclose. Tie with kitchen twine at 5cm intervals. Rub the pork generously with salt. Transfer to a roasting tin and roast for 15 minutes. Reduce the oven temperature to 180°C and roast for 1 hour. Allow to rest for 5 minutes, then slice and serve immediately.

Make sure you have a good butcher who will select your pork belly and score it for you. Rolling and tying the pork belly on your own can be tricky and you may need some assistance. Cut your kitchen twine and have it at the ready before you start this process.

ROAST LAMB WITH CIDER VINEGAR

Serves 8

The flavours here are sensational – sweet carrots, delicate celery and lemon merge to give a refreshing yet robust finish on the palate. The other brilliant thing about this dish is the way the entire roast is cooked in one roasting pan, imparting every last drop of flavour.

2 tablespoons olive oil

2 onions, red or white, diced

2 carrots, roughly chopped

2 celery stalks, diced

2 whole garlic bulbs, halved

2 lemons, halved

1 x 1.2kg leg of lamb

2 bunches of Dutch carrots, trimmed and peeled

100g celery leaves (nice big ones), roughly chopped

150ml apple cider vinegar

80ml (⅓ cup) maple syrup

Preheat the oven to 180°C.

Heat the oil in a large roasting pan over medium–high heat. Add the onion, chopped carrot, celery and garlic and cook for 8 minutes, or until soft and lightly coloured. Squeeze the lemon juice into the pan and add the squeezed halves.

Season the lamb with salt and pepper, add to the pan and brown all over. Transfer the pan to the oven and roast for 40 minutes. Add the Dutch carrots, celery leaves, vinegar and maple syrup and cook for a further 40 minutes.

Set aside to rest for 5 minutes. Carve the lamb outside of the roasting pan, then return for serving.

PAELLA

Serves 4

There's no chorizo in my version of paella, but there's plenty of seafood. If you haven't got a paella pan bring out your favourite cast-iron pan and within 30 minutes you'll feel like you're in Portugal.

625ml (2½ cups) gluten-free chicken stock

pinch of saffron

1 tablespoon olive oil

1 small white onion or raddish, finely chopped

8 scallops

300g (1½ cups) biryani rice, store-bought

6–8 large green prawns, whole with shells on

200g white fish such as snapper or ling, cut into bite-size pieces

200g dark fish such as tuna, cut into bite-size pieces

zest and juice of ½ lemon

¼ cup flat-leaf parsley leaves

In a medium saucepan bring the stock to a simmer, add the saffron and set aside.

Heat the oil in a paella pan over medium heat. Add the onion and cook, stirring, for 5 minutes, or until translucent. Add the scallops, increase the heat to high and sear for 2–3 minutes on both sides until just brown. Remove the scallops from the pan and set aside.

Return the heat to low and add the rice to the pan, spreading the grains evenly, then add the stock. Gently simmer for 3–5 minutes, then add the prawns and scallops, placing them gently over the rice. Simmer for a further 3 minutes, then add the fish. Reduce the heat to medium–low and simmer gently for 5–8 minutes, until the stock is almost completely absorbed. Turn the seafood, very delicately using tongs, once during this process.

Remove from the heat and dress with the lemon zest and juice and parsley leaves. Season with salt and pepper and serve immediately.

Delicious biryani rice is tossed with small amounts of turmeric, cardamom, cinnamon, miniature lentils and one or two bay leaves. You can experiment with a combination of spices to create your own signature rice.

WHOLE BAKED SALMON WITH SMASHED PEAS, LEMON AND CHERVIL

Serves 4

A perfect spring or summer dinner jazzed up with fresh peas and the delicate flavour of one of my favourite herbs, chervil. Add a crisp salad and a glass of Riesling to lift this meal up another notch.

1 x 1kg side of salmon, pin bones removed

white pepper

450g (3 cups) shelled fresh peas or frozen peas

1 small spring onion, finely chopped

1 tablespoon finely chopped chervil leaves

zest and juice of 1 lemon

a splash of olive oil

Preheat the oven to 150°C. Line a large baking tray with baking paper, place the salmon on top and season with sea salt and white pepper. Bake for 25 minutes, or until cooked through.

Bring a medium saucepan of water to the boil, add the peas and cook for 5 minutes (a little less for frozen peas). Drain and cool slightly.

In a medium bowl combine the onion and chervil with the lemon zest and juice.

In a separate bowl or the saucepan, gently smash the peas with a fork or lightly press with a potato masher – don't turn them into a mash, just squash and break them. Add the smashed peas to the onion mixture, toss to combine and finish with a splash of olive oil.

Transfer the salmon to a serving platter, cut into four even portions and top with the smashed pea mixture. Season generously with ground black pepper and serve immediately.

VEGETABLE RISONI

Serves 6

Risoni isn't an entirely accurate description for this dish, which is basically a broth with risotto rice, but it resembles the minestrones and risonis I've envied from across the table in Italian restaurants and is just as satisfying. It reminds me of the transition from winter to spring – an excellent time to make this dish when broad beans are in season.

250g zucchini (I used white and green), finely chopped

100ml olive oil

2 onions, finely chopped

500g tomatoes, blanched in hot water and peeled

2 small potatoes, finely diced

½ cup broad beans

50g fine arborio rice

3 garlic cloves, crushed

a handful of roughly chopped basil leaves

2 egg yolks, beaten

Place the zucchini in a paper towel and squeeze to drain excess liquid.

In a medium to large saucepan heat the olive oil over medium heat, add the onion and cook, stirring, for 3 minutes, then add the zucchini and cook for 10 minutes.

Roughly chop all but two of the tomatoes and add to the zucchini and onion mixture. Cook for 5 minutes or until soft, add the potato and 1.25 litres of water and bring to a simmer. Add the broad beans and arborio rice and season with salt and pepper. Simmer for a further 5–7 minutes over low heat.

In the meantime, top the remaining two tomatoes with the garlic and basil and drizzle with olive oil. Grill for 5 minutes, or until tomatoes are aromatic and turning brown, then add to the rice mixture and stir gently to combine.

Slowly add the egg yolk to the risoni, one tablespoon at a time, stirring gently. Ladle the risoni into bowls, season with salt and pepper and serve.

Pastry, Pies, Pizza and Pasta

In business I have four Ps: passion, planning, product and persistence. And in cooking, when you're gluten-intolerant, pastry, pies, pizza and pasta are the four Ps you generally skip. Not anymore. This chapter shatters the mould, delivering gluten-free options that are just like the real deal.

TOMATO, ONION AND GOAT'S CHEESE TART

Serves 6

Yum! Yum! Amazing for lunch, dinner, a picnic – or even a sly snack. This tart stands on its own.

PASTRY

100g rice flour

2½ tablespoons gluten-free cornflour

2½ tablespoons fine polenta

½ teaspoon xanthan gum

½ teaspoon gluten-free baking powder

1 teaspoon salt

125g unsalted butter, chopped and chilled

200g cold mashed potato

1 tablespoon sesame seeds, toasted

filling (see recipe over page)

To make the pastry, pulse the flours, polenta, xanthan gum, baking powder and salt in a food processor to combine. Add the butter and pulse until the mixture resembles fine breadcrumbs. Transfer to a bowl, add the potato and sesame seeds and mix well with your hands until dough feels smooth and elastic. Knead the pastry for 2–3 minutes until smooth. Shape into a ball, cover with plastic wrap and refrigerate for 30 minutes.

Preheat the oven to 180°C. Lightly grease a 30 x 21cm loose-based flan tin.

Roll out the pastry to form a 32 x 23cm rectangle on a lightly floured surface. Press into the prepared tin, covering the sides and edges, and line the pastry shell with baking paper and pastry weights or uncooked rice. Blind bake for 15 minutes. Remove the baking paper and pastry weights and return the pastry case to the oven for a further 5–7 minutes, or until golden. Set aside to cool slightly.

 continued

TOMATO, ONION AND GOAT'S CHEESE TART

continued

FILLING

50g unsalted butter

1 tablespoon olive oil

2 large red onions, sliced

1 garlic clove, finely chopped

2 eggs

2 egg yolks

150ml cream

200g cherry tomatoes, halved

1 teaspoon chopped thyme, plus extra for garnishing

100g goat's cheese

Increase the oven to 200°C.

To make the filling, melt the butter and oil in a large frying pan over medium heat. Add the onion and garlic and cook, stirring, for 15 minutes, or until soft and golden. Season well with salt and pepper.

Whisk the eggs, egg yolks and cream in a large bowl. Stir in the onion mixture, tomato and thyme, then pour into the pastry case. Crumble the goat's cheese over the top and bake for 25 minutes, or until golden.

Garnish with the extra thyme, season with some more pepper and serve.

MUSHROOMS AND PUMPKIN IN VERY FLAKY PASTRY

Serves 4

This dish was inspired by pastry from an Indian snack. I have made a few tweaks to the pastry and combined it with a field of mushrooms and some pumpkin to make for a splendid autumn meal.

PASTRY

450g warm mashed potato

100g ghee*

175g (1 cup) rice flour

1 teaspoon salt

filling (see recipe over page)

To make the pastry, mix the mashed potato with the ghee in a large bowl. Work in the flour and salt and knead for 2–3 minutes until the dough comes together. Shape the dough into a disc, cover with plastic wrap and refrigerate for 1 hour.

Preheat the oven to 180°C. Lightly grease a 30cm pizza tray or a 12 x 34cm rectangular loose-based flan tin.

On a lightly floured work surface, roll out the pastry until 1cm thick to fit the size of the tray or tin. Press into the tray or tin and curl up the edges to create a side casing. Spread a thin layer of the chestnut puree over the pastry. Bake for 10–15 minutes, or until the sides are lightly golden.

* Ghee is clarified butter and is sometimes hard to locate. If you can't find it in your supermarket, head to your nearest Indian grocer.

 continued

MUSHROOMS AND PUMPKIN IN VERY FLAKY PASTRY

continued

FILLING

2 tablespoons chestnut puree

80ml (⅓ cup) olive oil

150g pumpkin, cut into small chunks

2 tablespoons water

50g butter

400g mixed mushrooms, such as field, portobello, button, oyster or shiitake, stems removed

1 tablespoon coarsely crushed macadamia nuts

3 thyme sprigs, plus extra for garnishing

2 garlic cloves, finely chopped

1 egg white, beaten

Heat 2 tablespoons of the oil in a large frying pan over medium heat. Add the pumpkin and cook, stirring, for 2 minutes. Pour in the water and cook for 2 minutes, or until the pumpkin is tender. Remove from the pan and set aside.

Wipe the pan clean and heat the remaining oil and the butter over medium heat. Add the mushrooms and macadamias and cook for 1–2 minutes. Season with salt and pepper. Stir in the thyme and garlic and cook for a further minute.

Increase the oven to 200°C. Combine the mushroom and pumpkin mixtures and drain the excess liquid. Spread the vegetable filling over the tart shell.

Brush the top of the tart with the beaten egg white, paying particular attention to the exposed pastry. Bake for 15–20 minutes, or until the pastry is golden brown.

Garnish with the extra thyme and serve immediately.

CHICKEN SOUP PIES

Serves 4

Having been a lifelong fan of the pie, there was a not so happy time when I just couldn't eat them, but with this ingenious crumbed crust the Saturday afternoon pie experience is mine again.

1.2kg skinless chicken breast fillets, diced

2 tablespoons gluten-free cornflour

100g butter

2 leeks, white part only, halved lengthways and thinly sliced

2 tablespoons chopped flat-leaf parsley, plus extra for garnishing

170ml (⅔ cup) milk

250ml (1 cup) cream

1 egg

BREADCRUMBS
Makes 1½ cups

65g (1 cup) golden rice flakes

30g (½ cup) shredded coconut

75g (½ cup) fine polenta

50g butter

To make the breadcrumbs, combine the rice flakes, coconut and polenta in a food processor and pulse until the mixture resembles coarse breadcrumbs. Alternatively, crush by hand between two sheets of baking paper. The crumbs should look rustic and not too fine. Transfer the crumbs to a bowl.

Melt the butter in a frying pan, pour over the crumbs and toss to combine. Set aside.

Preheat the oven to 180°C. Lightly grease four 310ml (1¼ cup) heatproof dishes (I used heart-shaped foil trays for this). Coat the chicken with the cornflour and season with the salt and pepper.

Melt the butter in a large frying pan over medium–high heat, stir in the leek and sweat for 3–5 minutes. Add the chicken and cook for 3 minutes until lightly brown. Remove from the heat and slowly stir in the parsley and milk. Return to the heat and simmer, stirring, for 3–5 minutes until the mixture has thickened and all the ingredients are combined and well coated.

Whisk the cream and egg in a small bowl and pour into the pan with the chicken and leek. Bring to a gentle simmer. Remove from the heat.

Spoon the chicken mixture into the prepared dishes and sprinkle on the reserved crumb mixture. Bake for 25 minutes, or until the crumb topping is golden. Serve warm, sprinkled with parsley.

QUICHE À LA ROWIE

Serves 6–8

This simple meal is a great midweek dinner solution after a busy day. Quiche was something I missed for years; walking past bakeries, staring sadly at their window displays and knowing I couldn't indulge was possibly one of the driving factors behind the creation of my business. And that's why I have renamed and reclaimed the quiche!

100g rice flour

2½ tablespoons gluten-free cornflour

1 teaspoon salt

½ teaspoon gluten-free baking powder

125g unsalted butter, chopped and chilled

200g cold mashed potato

150g thinly sliced prosciutto, torn

4 egg yolks

3 eggs

250ml (1 cup) cream

½ teaspoon freshly grated nutmeg

Preheat the oven to 180°C. Lightly grease a 23cm round fluted loose-based flan tin.

Sift the flours into a large bowl and, using your hands, mix in the salt, baking powder, butter and potato. Knead the pastry, pushing and folding it together for 3 minutes until pastry comes together in a ball.

Roll out the pastry between two sheets of baking paper to make a 30cm circle. Press into the prepared tin and line the pastry shell with baking paper and pastry weights or uncooked rice. Blind bake for 15 minutes. Cool slightly and remove the baking paper and weights. Reduce the oven temperature to 160°C.

Scatter the prosciutto over the pastry shell. Whisk the egg yolks, eggs, cream and nutmeg in a bowl and season with salt and pepper. Pour over the prosciutto and bake for 30–40 minutes, or until the filling is cooked through. Stand for 5 minutes – if you can help yourself – then serve.

HOMEMADE SAUSAGE ROLLS

Makes 8–10

The smells from the local patisserie used to send me wild while I daydreamed about the taste of a sausage roll. As a child sausage rolls were our weekly treat after a Saturday morning of sport and activity, and I would savour each and every bite. This recipe helps bring back that comforting taste with its crispy, crunchy pastry.

PASTRY

100g (¾ cup) quinoa flour, plus extra for dusting

100g (¾ cup) gluten-free cornflour

100g (⅔ cup) potato flour

125g butter, chopped and chilled

pinch of salt

1 egg

2–3 tablespoons water

1 egg white, beaten, for brushing

filling (see recipe over page)

Preheat the oven to 180°C. Line a baking tray with baking paper.

To make the pastry, place the flours, butter and salt in a bowl and rub in butter with your fingertips. Make a well in the centre and add the egg. Pour in the water and stir until the mixture forms a soft dough. Knead the dough on a lightly floured surface for 3 minutes, or until smooth. Roll out the pastry to form a 20 x 30cm rectangle.

To make the filling, combine the minces, eggs, tomato paste, chilli sauce, mustard, parsley and coriander in a large bowl.

Place a third of the mince mixture along one long side of the pastry. Brush the rest of the pastry with some of the egg white and gently roll, using a third of the pastry, around the filling to form a sausage shape. Using a palette knife, cut this section away from the rest of the pastry. Repeat twice with the remaining mince and pastry, making 3 rolls of even size.

continued

HOMEMADE SAUSAGE ROLLS

continued

FILLING

150g pork mince

150g chicken mince

150g lamb mince

2 eggs

3 teaspoons tomato paste

1 tablespoon gluten-free sweet chilli sauce

2 teaspoons wholegrain mustard

1 tablespoon chopped flat-leaf parsley

1 tablespoon chopped coriander

Brush the top of the rolls with egg white and make 3 score lines in each roll, cutting a third of the way through with a palette knife, so you have 4 small sausage rolls marked in each long roll.

Move the rolls to the prepared baking tray and bake for 35 minutes, or until the pastry is golden. Remove from the oven, allow to cool for 5 minutes, then cut into individual portions and serve.

TRADITIONAL PIZZA

Serves 6

My cousin Nicholas, also gluten-intolerant, loves his pizza so this recipe is for him. Some pizzerias now offer gluten-free bases, but nothing beats homemade, where you get to choose your topping and put it on just the way you like it.

BASE

65g (½ cup) buckwheat flour

55g (½ cup) soy flour

90g (½ cup) rice flour

2 teaspoons gluten-free baking powder

40g unsalted butter, chopped and softened

125ml (½ cup) water

2 egg yolks

TOPPING

4 tomatoes, thinly sliced

6 anchovy fillets

100g mozzarella cheese, sliced

a handful of basil leaves

1 tablespoon olive oil

Preheat the oven to 220°C. Grease a 30cm pizza tray.

Sift the flours and baking powder into a bowl. Rub in the butter with your fingertips until the mixture resembles coarse breadcrumbs. This can also be done with the aid of a food processor.

Combine the water and egg yolks in a small jug and mix well. Pour into the dry ingredients and mix with your hands to form a firm dough.

Turn the dough out onto a lightly floured surface and knead until it comes together in a ball. Roll out to form a 5mm-thick disc to fit the base of the pizza tray.

Place the dough on the pizza tray and press into position. Arrange the tomato slices on top of the pizza and season with salt and pepper. Scatter on the anchovies, mozzarella and basil leaves and drizzle with the olive oil. Bake for 20 minutes, or until the mozzarella is golden brown. Slice with a pizza cutter and serve immediately.

OH MY GOSH, PASTA!

Serves 6 (Yield: 1.3kg)

The trick to making this pasta is to work it – you really have to knead it firmly for the best results. It requires patience and dedication, but if you take the time to do this you'll soon enjoy digging in to some well-deserved and tasty pasta. Once you've got the hang of it, play around and try out some different shapes.

250g (2 cups) gluten-free cornflour

140g (1 cup) potato flour

300g (2 cups) fine polenta, plus extra for dusting

3 eggs

11 egg yolks

185ml (¾ cup) soda water

Sift the flours and polenta into a large bowl. Make a well in the centre and add the eggs, gently working them in with your hands. Make another well, add the egg yolks and work them into the mixture, adding a little soda water, a tablespoon at a time, until the mixture comes together to form a firm elastic ball.

Place the dough on long a sheet of baking paper, lightly dusted with a little of the extra polenta. Knead the pasta firmly with the heel of your hand for 3 minutes. Shape the dough into a log and divide into 6 portions. Loosely cover 5 portions with plastic wrap.

Place one portion of the dough on the floured baking paper, lightly dust the top and, using a rolling pin, firmly but gently roll out evenly until about 3mm thick. Set aside and repeat this process with the remaining portions of dough.

Using a palette or kitchen knife, cut the dough lengthways into 1cm wide strips, or desired width. Cook immediately in a large pot, in batches (don't overcrowd the pot), in salted and simmering water (that has just been turned down from boiling) with a few drops of olive oil for 3–5 minutes, or until al dente. Drain and serve with your favourite pasta sauce.

LASAGNE

Serves 6

My mother was the queen of comfort food and lasagne was one of her specialties. When we were doing rehearsals for our highschool musical my sisters and I would smile with glee when our friends would ask, 'Is Lynnie bringing her lasagne for dinner?' This vegetarian lasagne bakes beautifully and can be made a day ahead.

9 x lasagne sheets (see pasta recipe on page 90)

60ml (¼ cup) olive oil

3 garlic cloves, finely chopped

5 large tomatoes, blanched in hot water, peeled and diced

1 white onion, finely chopped

6 large spinach leaves, shredded

½ teaspoon nutmeg, plus extra for sprinkling

250g Swiss brown mushrooms, finely sliced with stalks on

⅓ cup sage leaves, roughly chopped

125ml (½ cup) gluten-free vegetable stock

80g (¾ cup) Parmesan or Pecorino, finely grated (for dairy-free use a hard soy cheese)

Preheat the oven to 200°C. Lightly grease a 35 x 25cm baking dish.

Follow the pasta recipe on page 90 until you have rolled out the pasta dough. Cut it into 8 x 11cm rectangles to make the lasagne sheets and set aside on baking paper.

Heat 1 tablespoon of the oil in a heavy-based saucepan over medium heat, add the garlic and cook for 3 minutes, or until the garlic is soft. Add the tomato and simmer for 6–8 minutes, stirring occasionally. Remove from heat and set aside.

Heat 1 tablespoon of the oil in a medium saucepan over medium heat, add the onion and sweat for 3–5 minutes, until translucent. Add the spinach, cover saucepan and cook over medium–low heat for 3 minutes. Sprinkle with the nutmeg and stir, then remove from heat and set aside.

Heat the remaining tablespoon of oil in a heavy-based saucepan over medium heat, add the mushroom and sweat for 5 minutes, stirring occasionally. Add the sage and vegetable stock and bring to a simmer. Remove from heat and set aside.

 continued

LASAGNE

continued

BÉCHAMEL SAUCE

800ml rice milk

2 tablespoons gluten-free cornflour, sifted

To make the béchamel sauce, pour the rice milk into a small to medium saucepan and gently warm, but do not bring to the boil, over a low heat for approximately 3 minutes. (Rice milk is water based so it will separate when you add the cornflour if the milk is too hot.) Whisk the cornflour into the rice milk, a teaspoonful at a time, add the cheese and continue to whisk. As soon as the sauce begins to thicken remove it from the heat and sprinkle with a little nutmeg. Stir gently again with a whisk and set aside.

To assemble the lasagne, spread the tomato mixture evenly over the base of the prepared baking dish. Cover with a layer of pasta and a third of the béchamel sauce. Top with the spinach mixture and sprinkle with a little extra nutmeg. Cover with a layer of pasta, spread with another third of the béchamel sauce and top with the mushroom mixture including the stock. Cover with a third layer of pasta, spread with the remaining béchamel sauce and sprinkle generously with Parmesan.

Reduce the oven to 180°C and bake for 30 minutes, or until golden on top. Remove from the oven and leave to stand for 5 minutes. Serve with a fresh garden salad.

PASTA SAUCES

Here are some simple, tasty and easy-to-create sauces that will dress up your pasta with colour and flavour. The colours are the same as Italian traffic lights: red, yellow and green.

BASIL WITH PINE NUTS AND GARLIC

2 tablespoons olive oil

2 garlic cloves, chopped

2 large handfuls of basil leaves

40g (¼ cup) pine nuts, toasted

TOMATO PASSATA

6 large vine-ripened tomatoes

½ teaspoon brown sugar

LEMON, OLIVE OIL AND MACADAMIA

2 tablespoons olive oil

500ml (2 cups) gluten-free chicken stock

zest of 2 lemons

70g (½ cup) toasted and finely crushed macadamia nuts

Basil: Heat the olive oil in a small saucepan over low heat, add the garlic and sweat for 3 minutes.

Meanwhile, combine the basil leaves and pine nuts in a food processor and pulse to form a coarse paste. Add the garlic and pulse again to combine. Return the basil mixture to the pan and cook over medium heat for 3 minutes. Serve immediately with pasta.

Tomato: Place the tomatoes in a heatproof bowl and pour in enough boiling water to cover. Set aside for 5 minutes. Drain and, when cool enough to handle, peel the tomatoes with a small sharp knife. Core the tomatoes and chop, retaining the juice and pulp.

Transfer the tomatoes, pulp and juice to a food processor and puree. Pour the puree into a small saucepan, add the sugar, stir, and simmer over medium heat for 5–7 minutes until gently bubbling. Season with salt and pepper and serve immediately with pasta. You can store passata for up to 5 days in an airtight container in the fridge.

Lemon: Heat the olive oil in a small saucepan over medium heat. Add the stock, bring to the boil and simmer for 5 minutes. Stir in the lemon zest and macadamias, season with salt and pepper and simmer for a further 2 minutes. Pour the sauce over pasta, toss well and serve immediately.

GNOCCHI WITH SAGE AND PINE NUTS

Another reason to move to Italy forever – this hearty potato dish with soothing buttered sage is pure contentment. I like to serve this on a big platter when I have guests, allowing people to tuck in when they feel like it.

3 (approx 600g) sebago potatoes

2 red onions, roughly chopped

1 garlic clove, whole

olive oil, for drizzling

90g (⅔ cup) quinoa flour

1 egg

100g (1 cup) Parmesan, grated

pinch of nutmeg

6 tablespoons butter or dairy-free margarine

⅓ cup sage leaves

a handful of pine nuts, toasted

Preheat the oven to 180°C. Grease and line a baking tray.

Wash and peel the potatoes and boil in lightly salted water. Drain and leave to cool, then mash and set aside.

Place the onion and garlic in the prepared baking tray, drizzle generously with oil, season with salt and pepper and bake for 15 minutes, or until softened and starting to golden.

Combine the mashed potato with the onion, garlic (remove skin after roasting), quinoa flour, egg, Parmesan and nutmeg, season wth salt and pepper and mix with your hands until well combined.

Form the dough into 1 tablespoonful balls. Bring a large saucepan of salted water to the boil. Drop 3–4 gnocchi at a time into the water, lower the heat to a simmer and cook for 3–4 minutes, until the gnocchi rises to the surface. Remove with a slotted spoon and keep warm while you cook the rest of the gnocchi in batches.

To make the sage butter, melt the butter in a saucepan over medium heat. Add the sage and a pinch of salt. Cook for 3 minutes until the sage leaves are starting to turn golden.

Place the gnocchi onto plates, pour the sage butter over the top and sprinkle with the toasted pine nuts.

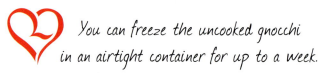

You can freeze the uncooked gnocchi in an airtight container for up to a week.

Big Cakes, Little Cakes

We all like a little – or a lot – of indulgence on occasion and this chapter delivers it in buckets! Leave your pre-conceived ideas about gluten-free baking behind and get ready for something akin to a religious conversion when you sample these delectable goodies. Taste, texture, method and presentation unite to bump the bland out of gluten-free cakes forever. Have fun baking!

DECADENT CHOCOLATE MOUSSE CAKE

Serves 10–12

Send your guests to epicurean heaven with this luxurious mousse-like cake that sets further on cooling. At Rowie's Cakes we produce a similar cake that is encrusted with coconut and palm sugar.

340g dark chocolate (70% cocoa solids), chopped

225g unsalted butter, chopped

5 eggs

210g caster sugar

100ml water

250g raspberries

Preheat the oven to 120°C. Grease and line a 20cm round cake tin.

Melt the chocolate and butter in a heatproof bowl over a saucepan of simmering water (do not let the bowl touch the water).

Beat the eggs and 70g of the sugar in a bowl with electric beaters for 8 minutes, or until tripled in volume.

Combine the remaining sugar and the water in a saucepan over medium heat and stir until the sugar has dissolved. Pour into the melted chocolate and set aside to cool slightly. If the mixture goes lumpy, give it a stir.

Fold the chocolate mixture into the egg mixture and beat slowly until smooth. Pour into the prepared tin.

Place a folded tea towel in a large roasting tin. Place the cake tin on top and add enough water to reach three-quarters of the way up the side of the tin. Bake for 1 hour, or until set – it should be bouncy and firm but still a little sticky. Cool in the water.

Gently turn out onto a serving plate when completely cool. Decorate the cake with the raspberries and serve.

DELICATE FEATHERY SPONGE

Serves 8–10

This is my take on the perfect sponge. To achieve the necessary light and feathery texture, fold the creamed mixture into the whites gently, so that you don't squash all the air out. The result is absolutely divine!

9 eggs, separated

350g (1½ cups) caster sugar

juice of 1 lemon

200g gluten-free cornflour

ICING

375g (3 cups) pure icing sugar

zest and juice of 1 lemon

zest and juice of 1 lime

Preheat oven to 180°C. Grease and line a 20cm round cake tin.

Place the egg yolks, caster sugar and lemon juice in a large bowl and beat with electric beaters on high speed for 5–8 minutes until the mixture is pale and thick. Sift in the cornflour and gently beat on low speed for up to 2 minutes, until the mixture is pale and creamy and the sugar has dissolved.

Beat the egg whites in a very large bowl until stiff peaks form. Pour the egg yolk mixture into the egg whites and fold in gently with a spatula, drawing the egg yolk mixture up into the egg white mixture.

Pour into the prepared tin and bake for 35–45 minutes, until golden on top or when skewer inserted into the centre comes out clean. Cool in the tin for 20 minutes.

To make the icing, sift the sugar into a bowl. Add the lemon and lime zest and juice and stir until lump free. If the icing is too thick, add a tablespoon of water, a few drops at a time, until the consistency of thickened cream (so it coats your cake and is not translucent).

Turn the cake out onto a cake stand or serving plate and pour the icing over the top, allowing it to randomly run down the side.

ORANGE AND CARDAMOM SYRUP CAKE

Serves 8

Moist and Moorish, this beautiful cake just oozes sophistication.

2 unpeeled oranges

200g silken tofu

1 teaspoon ground cardamom

250g (1¾ cups) palm sugar, grated or whizzed in a food processor

125ml (½ cup) olive oil

400g (4 cups) almond meal

zest of 1 lemon

zest of 2 oranges

1 teaspoon gluten-free baking powder

SYRUP

500ml (2 cups) strained orange juice

250g (1¾ cups) palm sugar, grated

Preheat the oven to 180°C. Grease and line a 22cm springform cake tin.

Boil the unpeeled whole oranges, covered in water, in a medium saucepan for 1 hour. Discard the water and set the oranges aside to cool. Cut open, remove pips and roughly chop 1½ oranges (discard the remaining half). You can prepare the oranges a day ahead if you wish.

Blend the oranges, silken tofu, cardamom, palm sugar and oil in a food processor until smooth and set aside. Combine the almond meal, lemon and orange zest and baking powder in a large bowl.

Fold the blended ingredients into the dry ingredients; the mixture will be fairly wet. Pour the batter into the prepared tin and bake for 1 hour and 10 minutes. Check after 45 minutes. If the cake is getting too dark on top, cover with foil. Cool completely before removing from the tin.

To make the syrup, combine the orange juice and sugar in a saucepan and cook over medium–high heat, without boiling, until the sugar dissolves. Then boil for 15 minutes until the syrup is thick and dark. Pour over the cake and serve.

LEMON AND SAFFRON TEACAKE

Serves 6

This exotic teacake will be the envy of many. The mix of saffron and lemon and the nutty flavour of quinoa pull together to provide a very decadent experience. High tea just got that bit more alluring!

¼ teaspoon saffron threads, lightly crushed

125ml (½ cup) soy milk, warmed but not boiled

125g unsalted butter, chopped and softened*

200g caster sugar

3 eggs

50g (½ cup) almond meal

1 teaspoon gluten-free baking powder

185g quinoa flour

zest of 1 lemon

80ml (⅓ cup) lemon juice

pure icing sugar, sifted, for dusting

Combine the saffron and soy milk in a small bowl, stir and set aside to infuse for 15 minutes.

Preheat the oven to 180°C. Grease and line the base and side of a 20cm round cake tin with baking paper, extending 2cm over the side of the tin.

Cream the butter and caster sugar in a large bowl with electric beaters until pale and fluffy (the sugar needs to dissolve and the mixture should be very creamy). Add the eggs, one at a time, beating well after each addition.

Sift the almond meal, baking powder and quinoa flour into a bowl and lightly combine with a whisk. Add a third of the flour mixture to the creamed mixture, folding through with a spoon. Add half the lemon zest and juice and fold. Add another third of the flour mixture and the remaining lemon zest and juice and fold. Add the remaining flour mixture and the soy milk and saffron mixture, continuing to fold through until completely combined.

Spoon the batter into the prepared tin and bake for 45 minutes, or until a skewer inserted in the centre of the teacake comes out clean. Cool the cake in the tin for 10 minutes before turning out onto a wire rack to cool completely. Dust the teacake with the icing sugar and serve.

* To make a dairy-free cake, use a dairy-free margarine in place of the butter.

LIME AND COCONUT ISLAND CAKE

Serves 8

This is my islander cake. It conjures up images of the Bahamas – big swinging banana leaf fans, rattan armchairs and clear blue water as far as you can see. Best consumed with a laidback island attitude and a Long Island Iced Tea.

150g unsalted butter, chopped and softened
230g (1 cup) caster sugar
5 eggs
140g (1¼ cups) coconut flour
1½ teaspoons gluten-free baking powder
150g (1¾ cups) desiccated coconut
430ml (1¾ cups) buttermilk

SYRUP

230g (1 cup) caster sugar
zest and juice of 1 lemon
zest and juice of 1 lime
125ml (½ cup) water

ICING

2 egg whites
2 teaspoons lemon juice
375g (3 cups) pure icing sugar, sifted

Preheat the oven to 175°C. Grease and line a high-sided (approx 9.5cm) 20cm springform cake tin. Cream the butter and sugar in a large bowl with electric beaters until pale and fluffy (the sugar needs to dissolve and the mixture should be very creamy). Add the eggs, one at a time, beating well after each addition.

Sift the coconut flour and baking powder into a separate bowl and mix in the desiccated coconut with a whisk. Fold the coconut mixture and the buttermilk into the egg mixture. Pour the batter into the prepared tin and bake for 1 hour, or until firm on top. Cool in the tin on a wire rack.

To make the syrup, place all the ingredients in a medium saucepan and bring to the boil, stirring, until the sugar is dissolved. Reduce the heat to medium–low and simmer for 10–15 minutes without stirring. Pour one third of the syrup over the cake in the tin. After 5 minutes pour over another third of the syrup. If your cake still needs more liquid, after a further 5 minutes, pour over the remaining syrup being careful not to add more than it can absorb. Set the cake aside for at least 3 hours or overnight.

To make the icing, beat the egg whites and lemon juice with electric beaters until stiff peaks form. Gradually add the sugar and beat until the icing is thick and holding perfectly smooth and shiny 'standing' peaks. Be very careful not to overbeat, this will cause the icing to break down into clumps. Using a palette knife, quickly (the icing sets very fast) and evenly spread the icing over the entire cake to create peaks all over the top and sides.

BERRY RICOTTA CAKE

Serves 8

The butterscotch and almond-berry flavour of this cake makes it one of my all-time favourites. It is beautiful, but be warned, it is very, very addictive. I have had friends eat one, two or even three slices in a sitting. You will love it!

150g unsalted butter, chopped and softened

230g (1 cup, firmly packed) brown sugar

1 vanilla bean, split lengthways and seeds scraped

2 eggs

150g smooth ricotta

65g (½ cup) quinoa flour

1 teaspoon gluten-free baking powder

50g (½ cup) almond meal

100g raspberries or frozen mixed berries

90g (1 cup) flaked almonds

pure icing sugar, sifted, for dusting

Preheat the oven to 180°C. Grease and line a 20cm springform cake tin.

Cream the butter, sugar and vanilla seeds with electric beaters until pale and fluffy. Add the eggs, one at a time, beating well after each addition. On low speed, beat in the ricotta until just combined. Fold in the quinoa flour, baking powder and almond meal with a large spoon.

Spoon the batter into the prepared tin. Smooth the top and scatter on the berries and flaked almonds. Cover with foil and bake for 50–55 minutes, or until a skewer inserted into the centre comes out clean.

Cool in the tin for 15–20 minutes, then turn out onto a wire rack to cool completely. Dust the top with icing sugar and serve.

COCOA SPONGE CAKES

Makes 6

Scrumptious and simple, these cakes are free of most ingredients that cause allergic reactions. The secret's all in the method: the volcanic reaction of the vinegar explodes to create your 'egg'. Remember that fabulous childhood drink, the Spider? It's a little like what happens when you drop a scoop of ice-cream into the lemonade.

195g (1½ cups) quinoa flour

40g (⅓ cup) gluten-free cocoa powder

1 teaspoon gluten-free baking powder

230g (1 cup) caster sugar

125ml (½ cup) vegetable oil

250ml (1 cup) coffee, chilled

2 teaspoons vanilla extract

2 teaspoons white vinegar

ICING

125g dairy-free margarine

155g (1¼ cups) pure icing sugar

½ tablespoon gluten-free cocoa powder

Preheat the oven to 190°C. Grease and line six mini loaf tins (10 x 6.5cm) or line a 12-hole standard muffin tin with paper cases.

Mix the flour, cocoa, baking powder and sugar in a large bowl.

Combine the oil, coffee and vanilla in a separate bowl, then add to the dry ingredients and stir well. Add the vinegar and quickly stir to combine (this will help the mixture to rise when baked). Don't let the mixture sit, pour immediately into the loaf tins or paper cases. Bake for 25–30 minutes, or until a skewer inserted into the middle comes out clean. Cool in the tin and turn out onto a wire rack for icing.

To make the icing, beat the margarine and sugar in a small bowl with electric beaters until well combined. Add the cocoa powder and beat until well combined and the icing is smooth and thick. Using a palette knife, spread the icing generously over the cakes, creating lines and patterns if you like.

POLENTA HEART CAKES

Makes 20

Dietary requirements or not, everyone needs a little love. I used heart-shaped silicone moulds to bake these cute cakes.

270g butter, chopped and softened

270g caster sugar

finely grated zest of 3 lemons

4 eggs

130g (1¼ cups) almond meal

130g (2 cups) shredded coconut

130g fine polenta

1 teaspoon gluten-free baking powder

juice of 2 lemons

ICING

250g (2 cups) pure icing sugar

juice of 1 lemon

2 teaspoons water, if needed

Preheat the oven to 160°C. Grease twenty 80ml (⅓ cup) silicone heart moulds or silicone muffin moulds. Cream the butter, sugar and lemon zest in a large bowl using electric beaters until pale and fluffy. Add the eggs, one at a time, beating well after each addition.

Combine the almond meal, coconut, polenta and baking powder in a separate bowl.

Fold the dry ingredients and the lemon juice into the creamed mixture. Pour the batter into the moulds and bake for 30–40 minutes until a skewer inserted into the middle comes out clean. Allow the cakes to cool completely in the moulds, then turn out ready for icing.

To make the icing, sift the sugar into a bowl, add the lemon juice and stir with a fork to completely combine. The icing should be gently runny so you may need to add a little water. Spread the icing over the cakes and leave to dry, then transfer the iced heart cakes to colourful paper cases and let the love shine in!

ALMOND, ROSEWATER AND CHERRY CAKES

Makes 8

Very Middle Eastern and very delicate. To obtain a stronger almond flavour, replace the rosewater with almond essence.

250ml (1 cup) vegetable oil

345g (1½ cups) caster sugar

2 eggs

250g (1 cup) natural yoghurt or soy yoghurt

130g (1 cup) quinoa flour

100g (1 cup) almond meal

2 tablespoons rosewater

125g (1 cup) pure icing sugar, sifted

2–4 teaspoons warm water

a handful of halved and pitted cherries, for decoration

Preheat the oven to 180°C. Grease eight 250ml (1 cup) decorative non-stick moulds.

Combine the oil, caster sugar and eggs in a bowl and beat well with electric beaters. Stir in the yoghurt, then mix in the flour and almond meal. Stir in half the rosewater and divide the mixture among the moulds. Bake for 25–30 minutes, or until a skewer inserted into the middle comes out clean.

Cool slightly in the moulds for 5–10 minutes, then turn the cakes out onto a wire rack to cool completely.

To make the icing, place the icing sugar and the remaining rosewater in a bowl. Using a wooden spoon, gradually stir in enough water to make a smooth, flowing icing.

Pour the icing on the cakes and decorate with the cherries. For a more dazzling look, leave the stalks on the cherries.

STRAWBERRY SHORTCAKES

Makes 6

This is such a classic recipe. The key is picking meaty strawberries that will make your mouth tingle with delight when combined with the vanilla and ricotta cream.

200g (2 cups) almond meal

75g (¾ cup) skim milk powder

65g (¾ cup) desiccated coconut

90g (½ cup) rice flour

2 teaspoons gluten-free baking powder

250ml (1 cup) rice milk

500g ricotta

1 teaspoon vanilla extract

2 tablespoons pure icing sugar

500g strawberries, hulled and diced

160g (½ cup) strawberry jam, warmed (optional)

Preheat the oven to 170°C. Grease six 12cm loose-based flan tins.

Combine the almond meal, skim milk powder, coconut, rice flour and baking powder in a large bowl. Add the rice milk and stir. Spoon the mixture into the prepared tins and press into the base and sides. Bake for 20–25 minutes until golden and cooked through. Cool completely in the tins.

Blend the ricotta, vanilla and sugar in a food processor until smooth. Spread over the shortcake base, then top with the strawberries. You can drizzle some warmed jam over your shortcakes to serve, but if your strawberries are juicy enough, you may not need to.

CHOCOLATE SOUFFLÉS

Makes 4

Treat yourself with these divine choccie soufflés. Timing is everything with these, so get the best results by prepping the mixture five minutes after dinner. Eat immediately, with a real silver spoon!

100g caster sugar, plus extra for dusting

40g (⅓ cup) gluten-free cocoa powder

1 tablespoon instant coffee

80ml (⅓ cup) water

6 egg whites

pinch of cream of tartar

Preheat the oven to 190°C. Grease four 250ml (1 cup) ramekins and dust the inside with a little extra caster sugar.

Place the cocoa, coffee and water in a saucepan and stir over low heat until dissolved. Increase the heat to medium–high and simmer for 2 minutes. Set aside to cool for 5 minutes.

Whisk the egg whites until soft peaks form. Add the caster sugar and cream of tartar and continue to beat until stiff peaks form. Gently fold a little of the egg white mixture into the mocha mixture, then fold the mocha mixture into the remaining egg whites until just combined.

Spoon the mixture into the prepared ramekins, filling to the top. Transfer to a baking tray and bake for 10–12 minutes, or until risen. Serve immediately.

treat yourself

The Sweetest Things

I have a confession to make. I actually art direct desserts like a costume designer does with gowns in a movie. I love the fact that you can create theatre at the table with stunning visual effects and a bit of imagination. It's a fitting encore to a fabulous main meal. Treat yourself to these heavenly goodies.

LEMON AND RICOTTA CHEESECAKE

Serves 10–12

This cheesecake is quite tart and not sweet at all, but it's the perfect match for a glass of dessert wine, so impress your friends with your skills in the art of food and wine matching. If you fancy a little sweetness, add ½ cup pure icing sugar to the ricotta mixture.

100g golden rice flakes

1kg ricotta

3 eggs

2 egg whites

zest and juice of 2 lemons

50g (⅓ cup) gluten-free cornflour

125g honey

Preheat the oven to 180°C. Grease and line a 20cm springform cake tin. Spread the rice flakes on a baking tray and bake for 5 minutes, or until crisp. Set aside to cool. Reduce the oven temperature to 140°C.

Place the ricotta, eggs, egg whites, lemon zest and juice, cornflour and honey in a food processor and blend until smooth.

Crush the rice flakes with a rolling pin and spread a thin layer in the base of the prepared tin. Spoon on the ricotta mixture, smooth the top and bake for 35–45 minutes, or until golden and set.

Allow to cool. Chill in the fridge for 2 hours or overnight.

NECTARINE TART

Serves 6

This is a beautiful recipe, similar to a tarte tatin, and the vibrant colours are like something out of an Impressionist painting. Picnic here we come…

PASTRY

65g (½ cup) quinoa flour

1 teaspoon ground cinnamon

65g unsalted butter, chopped

1 egg yolk

1 tablespoon water

TOPPING

6 large nectarines, halved, stoned and sliced

1 tablespoon caster sugar

½ teaspoon ground cinnamon

80g (¼ cup) apricot jam, warmed

Grease and line a baking tray.

To make the pastry, combine the flour, cinnamon, butter, egg yolk and water in a food processor and pulse for 15 seconds until the dough just comes together. Shape into a disc, cover with plastic wrap and refrigerate for 15 minutes.

Roll out the pastry on a lightly floured surface into a 2mm thick rectangle to fit the size of your baking tray, leaving a 2cm edge. Place on the prepared baking tray and crimp the edges neatly using your fingers. Return to the refrigerator for 15 minutes.

Preheat the oven to 200°C.

For the topping, cover the pastry with the nectarine slices, leaving a smidgen at the edge uncovered. Sprinkle with the sugar, dust with the cinnamon and bake for 30 minutes, or until the pastry is golden. Cool slightly and brush with the jam. Serve warm.

CLASSIC LEMON TARTS

Serves 4

There's nothing quite like the soothing taste of a subtle, crisp pastry with a gentle lemon curd. Quinoa flour has a rustic, earthy taste which gives a refreshing crispness to this pastry once combined with the sweet tartness of your lemon cream.

PASTRY

170g (1⅓ cups) quinoa flour

80g (⅔ cup) pure icing sugar, plus extra, sifted, for dusting

2 tablespoons almond meal

100g unsalted butter, chopped and chilled

1 egg, separated

1 teaspoon chilled water

FILLING

5 eggs

180g (¾ cup) caster sugar

finely grated zest of ½ lemon

juice of 2 lemons, strained

170ml (⅔ cup) cream

Lightly grease four 12cm round loose-based flan tins.

To make the pastry, pulse the flour, sugar and almond meal in a food processor until combined. Add the butter, egg yolk and water and pulse until the pastry just comes together. Keep working the dough in the food processor until well combined. It should be slightly sticky. Shape the dough into a disc, cover with plastic wrap and place in the fridge for 30 minutes.

Roll out the pastry to a thickness of 3mm on a lightly floured surface. Cut out four 14cm rounds and press into the prepared tins. Place the tins on a baking tray and chill in the fridge for 30 minutes.

Preheat the oven to 180°C. Line the pastry shells with baking paper and fill with pastry weights or uncooked rice. Blind bake for 12 minutes, or until the crust is golden. Carefully remove the baking paper and pastry weights. Lightly beat the egg white and brush the pastry cases. Return to the oven and bake for a further 3 minutes, or until the pastry cases are dry.

Reduce the oven temperature to 150°C.

To make the filling, whisk the eggs and sugar in a bowl until just combined. Stir in the lemon zest and juice and cream, then strain. Pour the filling into the pastry cases and bake for 35 minutes, or until the filling is just set. Cool the tarts in the tins. Remove the tarts from the tins, dust with the extra icing sugar and serve.

BLUEBERRY, MAPLE AND MASCARPONE TART

Serves 6

The big blue – blueberries and maple syrup with mascarpone is a fitting grand finale to any dinner party.

PASTRY

170g (1⅓ cups) buckwheat flour

100g unsalted butter, chopped and chilled

30g (⅓ cup) desiccated coconut

1 tablespoon pure icing sugar, plus extra, sifted, for dusting

3 tablespoons chilled water

FILLING

500g mascarpone

40g (⅓ cup) pure icing sugar

250g blueberries

100ml maple syrup

Grease a 10 x 34cm rectangular loose-based flan tin.

To make the pastry, pulse the flour, butter, coconut and sugar in a food processor to combine. Add the chilled water and pulse until the dough just comes together to form a ball.

Roll out the pastry to 2mm thick on a lightly floured surface. Line the prepared tin with the pastry and chill in the fridge for 20 minutes.

Preheat the oven to 180°C.

Line the pastry shell with baking paper and pastry weights or uncooked rice. Blind bake for 10 minutes until the pastry just starts to go golden on the edges. Carefully remove the baking paper and pastry weights. Return the pastry case to the oven for a further 10 minutes, or until golden and crisp. Set aside to cool on a wire rack.

To make the filling, process the mascarpone and icing sugar in a food processor until smooth.

Spoon the filling into the pastry case and smooth the top. Cover with the blueberries and drizzle with the maple syrup. Serve.

LAYERED MERINGUE CAKE WITH SEASONAL FRUIT

Serves 6–8

I adore meringue! I like it crisp on the outside and soft on the inside. Follow the instructions to creating a perfect meringue on page 136.

6 egg whites

300g caster sugar

pinch of salt

400ml thickened cream

2 tablespoons pure icing sugar, plus extra, sifted, for dusting

zest of 1 lime

500g seasonal fruit, such as mango passionfruit, raspberries, blueberries, bananas, pitted cherries, kiwi fruit and strawberries, diced or sliced (keep berries whole)

250g runny honey

Preheat the oven to 150°C. Line two baking trays with baking paper.

Whisk the egg whites in a large bowl with electric beaters on medium speed until stiff peaks form. With the beaters still whisking, gradually add the caster sugar and salt. Beat on high speed for 5–7 minutes until the meringue is thick and glossy. Divide the meringue mixture between the prepared trays and shape into 20cm circles. Bake for 45 minutes. Cool with the oven door ajar for 5 minutes, then transfer to a wire rack to cool completely.

Whip the cream and icing sugar until shiny soft peaks form. Fold in the lime zest at the very last minute to avoid curdling.

Place one meringue on a serving plate. Spoon on half the cream, top with half the fruit and drizzle on a little of the honey. Gently place the second meringue on top and spread on the remaining cream. Scatter on the remaining fruit and drizzle with the remaining honey. Dust with the extra icing sugar and serve. (I made a little extra meringue and placed a hat on top, then topped with some more fruit and honey.)

TIPS FOR CREATING THE PERFECT MERINGUE

Make sure your equipment is clean and dry.

Pour boiling water into the bowl and wipe it thoroughly dry before use.

When you separate the eggs, make sure there is no egg shell or remnants of egg yolk in with the egg white. The egg yolk contains fat and egg whites will not thicken if there is a trace of fat.

Sift the sugar before you start making the meringue.

Once your mixture is glossy and thick, don't let it sit around for long or the air will break down the stiff peaks and the meringue won't seal when it goes in the oven.

Know your oven well. Some ovens produce steam when cooking – it is best to cook meringue in a moisture-free oven. If your oven is steamy the meringue will cook but remain only semi-soft.

Cool your meringue away from a humid environment. Choose the coolest part of your house, out of the breeze and in the dark.

CHOCOLATE PAVLOVA

Serves 6

The complexity of the egg! Meringues are gorgeous and not that much of a challenge to create if you follow the tips on page 136. With a watchful eye you will soon become a master of the meringue and your friends and family will be clamouring at the kitchen door for more.

6 large egg whites

350g (1½ cups) caster sugar

1 teaspoon vanilla extract

3 tablespoons gluten-free cocoa powder, sifted, plus extra for dusting

Preheat the oven to 140°C. Line a baking tray with baking paper.

Whisk the egg whites in a large clean, dry bowl until soft peaks form. While continuously whisking, slowly add the sugar, a tablespoon at a time, until the mixture is thick and glossy. Beat in the vanilla.

Transfer half the mixture to another clean, dry bowl and gently fold in the cocoa.

Mound the white mixture into the centre of the prepared tray. Heap on the cocoa mixture and, using the back of a large clean, dry spoon, gently swirl the mixtures together to form a 6–8cm-high circle about 23cm in diameter. Bake for 1 hour and 15 minutes. (My pavlova has a soft marshmallowy centre. If you would like yours to be very, very crunchy, bake for a further 15 minutes.) Allow to cool in the oven with the door slightly ajar for 30 minutes.

Use spatulas to transfer your pavlova from the tray to a serving plate. Serve with a dramatic dust of cocoa powder. You could add some chopped raspberries on top, and for extra indulgence, serve with ice-cream.

TARTE TATIN

Serves 8

Invest in a good-quality cast-iron pan and start cooking and baking! Cast iron insulates and, for reasons I can't explain, it just makes a tarte tatin taste better. If you can't find a cast-iron pan, the next best thing is a ceramic baking dish.

150g unsalted butter, chopped and chilled
6–8 pink lady apples, cored and thinly sliced
250g caster sugar
2 whole cloves
½ vanilla bean, split lengthways and seeds scraped
150g rice flour
150g potato flour
100g (⅔ cup) instant polenta
1 teaspoon xanthan gum
250g brown sugar
1 egg
3 teaspoons water
1 egg white, beaten

Melt 20g of the butter in a large saucepan over medium heat. Add the apple, half the caster sugar, the cloves and vanilla seeds. Pour in just enough water to almost cover and bring to the boil. Reduce the heat to medium–low and simmer, stirring occasionally, for 5 minutes, or until the apple is translucent but not falling apart (we don't want apple sauce). Set aside to cool.

Preheat the oven to 160°C. Grease a 25cm cast-iron pan or baking dish. Sift the flours, polenta and xanthan gum into a large bowl. Use your fingertips to rub the remaining butter into the flour until the mixture resembles breadcrumbs. Mix in the brown sugar and the remaining caster sugar using your hands. Make a well in the centre, crack in the egg and, using your hands, slowly blend in the egg. Add the water and continue to mix with your hands until the dough just comes together.

Transfer the dough to a lightly floured work surface and knead until smooth. Flatten between two sheets of dusted baking paper and roll out until about 1cm thick and large enough to cover the top of your pan or dish.

Drain the fruit and spoon into the pan or dish. Place the pastry on top, trim to fit and press down around the edge to seal. Brush with the egg white and bake for 25 minutes. Reduce the temperature to 120°C and bake for a further 20 minutes, or until the pastry is golden brown. Set aside to cool for 15 minutes. Run a knife around the pastry edge, invert the tart onto a board, slice and serve.

SORBET SANDWICHED IN MELTING PASTRY

Makes 6

This melting pastry is like an old-fashioned brandy snap with that crispy, caramel taste. The sorbet can be made and devoured on its own, if desired.

80g unsalted butter, chopped

60g (⅓ cup, lightly packed) brown sugar

3 tablespoons golden syrup

2 teaspoons ground ginger

1 teaspoon lemon juice

1 tablespoon quinoa flour, sifted

30g (¼ cup) gluten-free cornflour, sifted

SORBET
Makes 1.5 litres

500g strawberries, hulled and thinly sliced

500g ripe bananas, peeled and thinly sliced

Line a large tray with baking paper.

To make the sorbet, arrange the thinly sliced fruit in a single layer on the prepared tray and place in the freezer for approximately 2 hours until half frozen. Place the half-frozen fruit in a food processor and process until thick and creamy. Transfer to an airtight container and return to the freezer for 1 hour.

Preheat the oven to 160°C. Grease two baking trays.

Combine the butter, sugar, 2 tablespoons of the golden syrup, the ginger and lemon juice in a saucepan over low heat and cook until the butter has melted. Remove from the heat and carefully stir in the flours until smooth.

Drop 12 well-spaced (2cm apart) teaspoons of the mixture onto the trays. Bake for 5 minutes, or until golden brown. Set aside to cool for 3–5 minutes, then slide the pastry rounds off the trays with a knife.

Sandwich scoops of the sorbet between two pastry rounds. Drizzle with the remaining golden syrup and serve immediately.

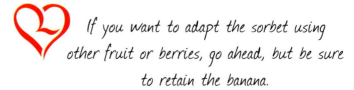

If you want to adapt the sorbet using other fruit or berries, go ahead, but be sure to retain the banana.

LEMON MERINGUE PIE

This reminds me of growing up and listening to my mother's stories about when she went to boarding school and the boring, stodgy food she ate there. How she looked forward to coming home to a lovely homemade pie like this one. Save this for a special occasion.

300ml milk

150ml cream

zest of 1 lemon

4 eggs, separated

1 egg yolk

175g (¾ cup) caster sugar

165g (2½ cups) golden rice flakes, crushed

500g (5 cups) almond meal

TRADITIONAL LEMON CURD
Makes 250ml (1 cup)

2 eggs

2 egg yolks

170g (¾ cup) caster sugar

80g unsalted butter, chopped and chilled

zest and juice of 2 lemons

To make the lemon curd, whisk the eggs, egg yolks, and sugar in a saucepan until pale, smooth and thick. Place the pan over low heat, add the butter and lemon zest and juice, and whisk continuously until thickened. Strain through a sieve into a bowl or sterilised jar.

Preheat the oven to 175°C. Lightly grease a high-sided (6cm) 20cm pie dish. Place the milk, cream and lemon zest in a saucepan over medium heat and bring to just below boiling point.

Combine the 5 egg yolks and 100g of the caster sugar in a bowl and beat with electric beaters until pale and creamy. On the lowest speed, carefully mix in the milk mixture, then add the rice flakes and almond meal. Spoon into the prepared dish and bake for 30 minutes, or until the pie crust is dry and golden. Set aside to cool.

Increase the oven temperature to 180°C. To make the meringue, whisk the egg whites in a large bowl until soft peaks form. Gradually add the remaining sugar, beating well after each addition, until thick and glossy.

Spread the lemon curd over the pie crust and top with the meringue, creating small peaks all over. Bake for 12–15 minutes, or until the peaks on the meringue are golden-tinged.

For best results, make your lemon curd the day before. Lemon curd can be prepared ahead and kept, covered, for up to 2 weeks in the refrigerator.

Bikkies, Slices and Snacks

Now, here's some snacks with personality.
In my world bikkies and slices aren't just boring fillers,
they are small treats to be savoured – morning,
noon or night. Enjoy!

THE MELTING MOMENT

Makes 24

These taste so good you will not believe that they are gluten-free. You will absolutely melt with glee the moment you bite into one.

375g unsalted butter, chopped and softened

185g (1½ cups) pure icing sugar

½ teaspoon vanilla extract

2 tablespoons honey

500g rice flour, plus extra for coating

ICING

150g butter or dairy-free margarine, chopped and softened

1 tablespoon milk

250g (2 cups) pure icing sugar

1 tablespoon passionfruit pulp

Preheat the oven to 160°C. Line a baking tray with baking paper.

Cream the butter, sugar, vanilla and honey in a large bowl with electric beaters until pale and fluffy. Add the rice flour and mix well.

Using lightly floured hands, roll the mixture into walnut-sized balls and place on the prepared tray. Gently flatten each ball with a fork dipped in some extra rice flour. Bake for 15 minutes, or until just golden. Remove from the oven and leave on the tray to cool.

To make the icing, beat the butter and milk until pale and creamy. Add the icing sugar gradually until well combined, then add the passionfruit pulp and combine well. When the biscuits are completely cooled, sandwich two 'moments' together with the passionfruit icing.

These bikkies can be stored in an airtight container in your fridge for up to 5 days.

MAPLE SLICE

Makes 12

This slice is liquid gold. If you're not fond of pecans, walnuts work just as well. To make a nut-free version, use sliced pineapple, plum or pear.

TOPPING

60g unsalted butter

60ml (¼ cup) maple syrup

80g (½ cup, lightly packed) brown sugar

100g (1 cup) pecans

BASE

120g unsalted butter

230g (1 cup) caster sugar

1 teaspoon vanilla extract

60g (½ cup) roughly chopped pecans

2 eggs, separated

195g (1½ cups) quinoa flour

2 teaspoons gluten-free baking powder

125ml (½ cup) milk

3 teaspoons instant coffee

Grease a 19 x 29cm slice tin.

To make the topping, place the butter, maple syrup and brown sugar in a small saucepan and stir over low heat until the butter has melted and the sugar has dissolved. Increase the heat to medium and continue to stir for 2 minutes, or until the mixture begins to caramelise. Pour into the prepared tin. Set aside to cool. When cool, arrange the pecans, rounded side down on top.

Preheat the oven to 170°C. To make the base, cream the butter and sugar in a large bowl with electric beaters until pale and fluffy. On low speed, mix in the vanilla and pecans. Add the egg yolks, one at a time, beating well after each addition.

Sift the quinoa flour and baking powder into a separate bowl. Add one-third of the flour mixture to the egg mixture, then add half the milk and mix well. Continue alternating the flour and milk until combined. Stir in the coffee.

Whisk the egg whites in another bowl until stiff peaks form. Fold the flour mixture, in batches, into the egg whites. Evenly pour the batter over the topping in the tin. Bake for 30 minutes, or until the slice comes away from the sides of the tin. Set aside to cool completely in the tin.

Run a knife around the edge of the tin. Invert the slice onto a serving plate and cut into 12 slices.

GOOEY DARK CHOC AND ORANGE BISCUITS

Makes 48

Simple and delightful! Little helpers will enjoy dipping the bikkies in chocolate and placing them on a wire rack to dry.

250g unsalted butter, chopped and softened

125g (1 cup) pure icing sugar

130g (1 cup) buckwheat flour

210g (1½ cups) brown rice flour

1 teaspoon finely grated orange zest

200g dark chocolate, broken into pieces

Preheat the oven to 170°C. Line two baking trays with baking paper.

Cream the butter and sugar in a large bowl using electric beaters until pale and fluffy. Add the flours and orange zest and beat on low speed until combined.

Turn the dough out onto a lightly floured surface and divide into two equal portions. Roll into two 25cm-long logs. Cover each log with plastic wrap and refrigerate for 30 minutes.

Cut each log into 1cm-thick slices and place the rounds 2cm apart on the prepared trays. Bake for 10–15 minutes until lightly golden. Leave on trays on a wire rack to cool completely.

Melt the chocolate in a heatproof bowl over a saucepan of simmering water (do not let the bowl touch the water). Set chocolate aside.

When the biscuits are cool, dip halfway into the melted chocolate and place on a wire rack until the chocolate has set. Store in an airtight container in the fridge for up to 5 days.

LEMON AND COCONUT MACAROONS

Makes 12

Ever heard of the meyer lemon? They have a sweeter, less acidic flavour than your average lemon. If you can get your paws on one, use the zest and these delicacies will be even more lemony and velvety when they land in your mouth.

2 large egg whites

2 tablespoons sugar

1 tablespoon finely grated lemon zest

a pinch of salt

105g (1¾ cups) shredded coconut

1 teaspoon potato starch

Preheat the oven to 160°C. Line a baking tray with baking paper.

Place the egg whites, sugar, lemon zest and salt in a bowl and stir to combine.

Toss the coconut with the potato starch.

Add the coconut mixture to the egg white mixture and mix well.

Using an ice-cream scoop, place 12 rounds of the macaroon mixture about 2cm apart on the prepared tray. Bake for 16–18 minutes, or until the tops are light golden brown.

STRAWBERRY RHUBARB LAYER WAFERS

Serves 8

This is a voluptuous take on a staple in the gluten-free pantry: puffed rice. Here's how to make puffed rice dance into the night.

½ bunch of rhubarb, trimmed and cut into 3cm lengths

325g strawberries, hulled and quartered

juice of ¼ lemon (approx 15ml)

150g mascarpone

25g (¼ cup) pure icing sugar, plus extra, sifted, for dusting

1 vanilla bean, split lengthways and seeds scraped

WAFERS

30g unsalted butter

150g white marshmallows

2 tablespoons honey

150g (5 cups) puffed rice

70g (½ cup) sesame seeds, toasted

Grease and line a 25 x 35cm baking tray.

To make the wafers, melt the butter in a saucepan over medium heat. Add the marshmallows, stir until melted, then mix in the honey. Combine the puffed rice and sesame seeds in a large bowl. Add the marshmallow mixture and stir until well combined. Pour onto the prepared tray and spread out evenly with a buttered spoon. Place a piece of baking paper on top and cover with something heavy like a phonebook or large cookbook. Set aside for 30 minutes.

Preheat the oven to 180°C. Place the rhubarb in a baking dish and bake for 20–25 minutes, or until tender.

Puree one-third of the strawberries with the lemon juice in a food processor and set aside.

Gently combine the rhubarb, the remaining strawberries and the strawberry puree in a bowl and set aside.

Combine the mascarpone, icing sugar and vanilla seeds in a bowl.

Using a 7cm round pastry cutter or an egg ring, cut out eight discs from the wafer and place on serving plates. Divide the mascarpone and vanilla cream between the wafer rounds, then top with the strawberry and rhubarb mixture. Dust with the extra icing sugar and serve.

LEMON AND GINGER BISCUITS

Makes about 20

Served with equal measures of pear and *fromage*, these biscuits will transport you to Paris. *Très bon!*

230g (1¾ cups) buckwheat flour

145g (⅔ cup) caster sugar, plus extra for dusting

½ teaspoon gluten-free baking powder

¼ teaspoon ground ginger

60g unsalted butter, cubed and chilled

2 eggs

3 teaspoons finely grated lemon zest

120g (1 cup) roughly chopped toasted hazelnuts

Preheat the oven to 180°C. Line two baking trays with baking paper.

Place the buckwheat flour, sugar, baking powder and ground ginger in a food processor and pulse for 2 seconds. Add the butter and pulse until the mixture resembles coarse breadcrumbs. Add the eggs and process until the dough just comes together.

Transfer the dough to a lightly floured surface (I generally use rice flour) and knead in the lemon zest and hazelnuts. Divide the dough into two equal portions. Shape each portion into a 20cm log. Place on the prepared trays and sprinkle with the extra sugar. Press down gently on the top of each log to flatten slightly. Bake for 20 minutes, or until golden.

Reduce the oven temperature to 160°C.

Cut the logs on the diagonal into 1cm-thick slices. Turn the baking paper over, then spread the biscuits on the trays in a single layer. Return to the oven and bake for 8–10 minutes, or until just beginning to turn golden on the edges. Cool completely before storing in an airtight container for up to 1 week.

DELICATE LAVENDER SHORTBREAD

Makes 24

These dainty biscuits are gorgeous for morning or afternoon tea. You can use fresh lavender if you have any available.

60g (½ cup) gluten-free cornflour

60g (½ cup) pure icing sugar, plus extra, sifted, for dusting

175g (1 cup) rice flour

170g butter, chopped and softened

1 teaspoon fresh edible lavender*

Preheat the oven to 150°C. Line two baking trays with baking paper.

Sift the cornflour, sugar and rice flour into a large bowl. Add the butter and lavender and mix with your hands until a soft dough forms. Shape into a disc, cover with plastic wrap and refrigerate for 1 hour.

Roll out the pastry on a lightly floured surface until 1cm thick. Using biscuit cutters, cut out shapes and place 3cm apart on the prepared trays. Bake for 20–25 minutes, or until the edges are lightly golden. Remove from the oven and cool completely on trays on a wire rack. Sift the extra icing sugar over the top. Store in an airtight container for up to 1 week.

* Edible lavender is available from selected gourmet providores or herb specialists.

MORNING SLICE

Makes 15 bars or squares

This is the best no-bake breakfast slice. It's easy, yummy and packed with fruit. To make this slice nut-free, replace the almonds with diced dried pineapple or pear.

100g (1 cup) quinoa flakes

3 tablespoons whole unblanched almonds

140g (¾ cup) dried apricots

90g dried apple

180g (1 cup) pitted dates

60g (½ cup) sultanas

2 dried figs

juice of ½ orange

Grease and line a 27 x 17cm slice tin.

Combine the quinoa, almonds and dried fruit in a food processor and pulse until completely combined. Add the orange juice a little at a time and pulse until the mixture lightly sticks together.

Press the mixture into the prepared tin. Refrigerate overnight, then cut into 15 bars or squares. Store in an airtight container in the fridge for up to 1 week.

PISTACHIO BISCOTTI

The opera finally comes to the bikkie tin!
These are amazing served with a lychee sorbet.

3 egg whites

2 tablespoons caster sugar

150g (1¼ cups) gluten-free cornflour

100g (½ cup) crystallised ginger, chopped

100g (¾ cup) crushed pistachio nuts

1½ teaspoons vanilla extract

Preheat the oven to 180°C. Grease a 9 x 16cm loaf tin and line the base and long sides with baking paper. Line a baking tray with baking paper.

Beat the egg whites in a large bowl until stiff peaks form. Gradually add the caster sugar and beat until the mixture is thick and glossy. Fold in the cornflour, ginger, pistachios and vanilla. Pour into the prepared tin and bake for 30 minutes, or until golden and firm to touch. Cool in the tin until ready to touch.

Reduce the oven temperature to 150°C. Cut the loaf lengthways into 1cm-thick slices, then cut each slice into 1cm-thick fingers. Place in a single layer on the prepared tray and bake for 10–15 minutes until crisp. Cool completely on the tray. Store in an airtight container for 4–5 days.

To make a lychee sorbet to accompany the biscotti, follow the recipe on page 142, replacing the strawberries with 500g pitted and halved lychees.

APPLE AND BERRY MINIETTES

Makes 12

A word on muffins: At Rowie's Cakes we refer to muffins as 'miniettes'. There's a delicacy and sweetness to these snacks that the word 'muffin' doesn't quite convey.

1 tablespoon gluten-free cornflour

440g (3⅓ cups) buckwheat flour

2 teaspoons bicarbonate of soda

2 apples, peeled and grated

180g (1 cup) dates, pitted and chopped

235ml maple syrup

375ml (1½ cups) water

300g fresh or frozen mixed berries

Preheat the oven to 180°C. Line a 12-hole standard muffin tin with paper cases.

Combine the cornflour, buckwheat flour and bicarbonate of soda in a large bowl. Add the apple, dates and maple syrup and gently mix together. Fold in the water with a large metal spoon. Lightly fold in the berries, being very careful not to break them, then spoon the mixture into the paper cases. Bake for 30 minutes, or until golden. Allow to cool in the tin for 5 minutes before transferring to a wire rack to cool completely. Serve with berry coulis, if desired.

MINT, GOAT'S CHEESE AND CHUTNEY MINIETTES

Makes 12

A great inbetween meals snack, these muffins are delicious served warm with chutney when eating at home or just as yummy when added to a lunchbox.

- 2 tablespoons potato starch
- 230g (1¾ cups) buckwheat flour
- 2 teaspoons gluten-free baking powder
- 30g (¼ cup) goat's cheese, crumbled, drained
- 25g (¼ cup) almond meal
- 2 eggs, beaten
- 250g (1 cup) sour cream
- 80ml (⅓ cup) vegetable oil
- 140g (½ cup) My favourite chutney (see recipe on page 169)
- 1½ tablespoons finely chopped mint

Preheat the oven to 180°C. Grease and line a 12-hole standard muffin tin.

Sift the potato starch, flour and baking powder into a bowl. Stir in the goat's cheese and almond meal. Add the eggs, sour cream and oil and mix to combine.

Half-fill each prepared mould with the muffin mixture, spoon in 1 teaspoon of the chutney, then fill to the top with the remaining muffin mixture. Bake for 10–12 minutes, or until golden. Cool for 5 minutes, then turn out onto a wire rack. Sprinkle with mint and drizzle with a spoonful of chutney. Keep, stored in an airtight container, for 3–4 days.

MY FAVOURITE CHUTNEY

Makes 1 cup

This is a must-have chutney for a barbecue and goes perfectly with gluten-free sausages or lamb cutlets. Gluten-free sausages are now readily available from gourmet butchers and supermarkets – forget those horror substitutes of the past, they taste a lot better now.

- a handful of mint
- 6 spring onions, roughly chopped
- 1 small red chilli, chopped
- 1 garlic clove
- 2 teaspoons raw sugar
- 1 teaspoon salt
- ½ teaspoon freshly grated nutmeg
- ½ teaspoon ground cinnamon
- juice of 2 lemons
- 2 tablespoons water

Combine all the ingredients in a food processor and process to form a puree. Spoon into a sterilised jar, seal and chill in the fridge. Keeps for 2–3 days.

WARM SPICED ONE-CUP PUDDINGS

Makes 6

Bring out your pudding pots for this toothsome winter and autumn treat.

125ml (½ cup) golden syrup, plus extra for drizzling

2 tablespoons potato flour

100g (¾ cup) quinoa flour

½ teaspoon bicarbonate of soda

½ teaspoon cream of tartar

175g butter, chopped and softened

3 eggs

½ teaspoon vanilla extract

185g (1 cup, loosely packed) brown sugar

½ teaspoon ground cinnamon

Grease and line six 250ml (1 cup) pudding basins or ovenproof tea cups. Spoon 1 tablespoon of the golden syrup into the base of each basin or cup.

Combine the flours, bicarbonate of soda and cream of tartar in a large bowl. Add the butter, eggs, vanilla, sugar, cinnamon and the remaining golden syrup and beat well. Spoon into the prepared basins or cups and secure the top of each with a sheet of foil. Place in two large saucepans and add enough boiling water to come halfway up the sides of the basins or cups. Cover the basins and cups with foil and boil for 50–60 minutes, or until your puddings are springy to touch. Set aside to cool for 5 minutes.

Drizzle with a little extra maple syrup and serve immediately in the basins or cups.

MELTING BANANA UPSIDE-DOWN PUDDINGS

Makes 6

When the first spoonful hits your mouth the banana and butterscotch flavours just melt on the tongue. Line your moulds delicately with banana to ensure your desserts are still looking picture perfect when you turn them out.

200ml maple syrup

160g butter, softened

80ml (⅓ cup) cream

3 ripe bananas

1 teaspoon lemon juice

220g (1¼ cups) raw caster sugar

2 eggs

1 vanilla bean, split lengthways and seeds scraped

300g (3 cups) almond meal

1 teaspoon bicarbonate of soda

1½ teaspoons ground cinnamon

80ml (⅓ cup) milk

Preheat the oven to 160°C. Grease six 250ml (1 cup) dariole moulds.

Place the maple syrup in a saucepan over medium–high heat and simmer for 8 minutes, or until starting to caramelise. Add 35g of the butter and the cream and swirl to combine. Remove immediately from the heat.

Pour 2 tablespoons of the caramel into the base of each prepared mould and swirl to coat the side. Reserve the remaining mixture.

Thinly slice 1 banana lengthways and layer the slices over the caramel. Set aside. Using a fork, mash the remaining bananas with the lemon juice (this should make about ¾ cup). Set aside.

Cream the remaining butter and the sugar in a large bowl with electric beaters until pale and fluffy. Add the eggs, mashed banana and the vanilla seeds and beat well.

Combine the almond meal, bicarbonate of soda and cinnamon, dust over the creamed mixture and stir well. Add the milk, in batches, and mix until smooth. Divide the mixture among the moulds, filling to 1.5cm below the rims (you may have a little mixture left over!). Bake for 20–25 minutes, or until risen and firm to touch. Turn out immediately onto serving plates (be patient as they may take a while to come out). Drizzle the reserved caramel over your upside-down puddings and serve.

The Entertainer

There's more to appetisers than dips and crackers. These recipes can be enjoyed before or after a meal or even at supper.

TARTLETS

Makes 12

These versatile tartlets can be used with sweet or savoury fillings. Make the bases and fill them with whatever you like. They are great for when guests arrive and much more exciting than a bowl of nuts!

75g rice flour

75g (½ cup) potato flour

75g (½ cup) fine polenta

1 teaspoon xanthan gum

pinch of salt

150g butter, chopped and chilled

1 egg, lightly beaten with 2 tablespoons water

Preheat the oven to 160°C.

Sift the flours, polenta, xanthan gum and salt into a bowl. Rub in the butter with your fingertips until the mixture resembles fine breadcrumbs. Make a well in the centre and pour in the egg and water mixture. Bring together with your hands to form a dough. If it is dry, you may need to add a little bit more water. Gather into a ball.

Knead the dough for 3–5 minutes on a lightly floured surface until silky. Flatten with the palm of your hand and roll out to a thickness of 5mm. Cut out 12 discs and gently press the pastry into 4cm round fluted tartlet tins. Line each pastry shell with baking paper and pastry weights or uncooked rice and blind bake for 20 minutes, or until golden. These tartlet shells keep well in an airtight container so you can prep ahead.

Recommended fillings

Sweet: go the ultimate and use lemon curd (see recipe on page 144)

Vegetarian: try a little mashed potato and dill, season with salt and pepper, curl some shaved asparagus on top and drizzle with a weeny bit of oil.

Outrageously decadent: whip some mascarpone, pipe into the shells and drop some caviar pearls on top.

HERBIE FLATBREAD

Makes 1 flatbread (8 pieces)

A savoury treat to make and store – I am sure you will want more! This bread is incredibly versatile – use it as a snack, an accompaniment to a meal or as a starter. Be creative and experiment with different herbs, salts and seeds to complement the earthy flavour of the flours.

65g (½ cup) buckwheat flour

55g (½ cup) soy flour

90g (½ cup) rice flour

2 teaspoons gluten-free baking powder

2 tablespoons softened unsalted butter

125ml (½ cup) water

2 egg yolks

a large handful of basil, rosemary and thyme leaves, finely chopped

1 tablespoon olive oil

Preheat the oven to 200°C. Grease a 30cm pizza tray.

Sift the flours and baking powder into a food processor. Add the butter and pulse until the mixture resembles fine breadcrumbs. Combine the water and egg yolks in a jug and pour down the chute of the food processor. Pulse until a firm dough forms.

Turn out onto a lightly floured surface and gently knead until smooth. Roll out the pastry to form a 30cm circle and transfer to the prepared tray. Sprinkle with the herbs and drizzle with the olive oil. Season with salt and pepper and bake for 20 minutes, or until golden. Cut into eight wedges and serve. You might like to try serving this with Tomato salsa (see page 184).

STUFFED DATES

Makes 12

These are a great dinner party starter. If you don't like goat's cheese, use a creamy sheep's cheese instead.

60g (½ cup) goat's cheese

3 tablespoons toasted pine nuts, plus extra to serve

1 teaspoon finely grated lemon zest

2 tablespoons lemon juice

½ teaspoon orange blossom water or ¼ teaspoon almond essence

12 large pitted dates

2 teaspoons ground sumac

2 tablespoons coriander leaves

a splash of extra virgin olive oil

Place the goat's cheese, pine nuts and lemon zest in a food processor and pulse to combine. Add the lemon juice and orange blossom water or almond essence, season with salt and pepper and pulse again until just combined.

Using a blunt knife, stuff the dates with the goat's cheese mixture and transfer to a platter. Dust with the sumac, scatter on the extra pine nuts and the coriander leaves, splash on the oil and serve.

TOFFEED NUTS

Serves 6–8

Perfect for relaxing with a coffee on a big fluffy lounge in front of the fireplace. Anyone for Scrabble?

575g (2½ cups) caster sugar

125ml (½ cup) water

50g butter

775g (5½ cups) mixed unsalted nuts, such as macadamias, walnuts, pistachios and almonds

Line a large baking tray with baking paper.

Combine the sugar and water in a large saucepan over medium heat and stir until the sugar dissolves. Bring to the boil, reduce the heat to low and simmer for 20–25 minutes until golden. Remove from the heat. Carefully add the butter and nuts and quickly pour onto the prepared tray. Set aside to cool. Break into pieces and serve. Store in the pantry in an airtight container for up to 10 days.

BRUSCHETTA

Serves 6–8

I can imagine you reading this and thinking, 'Wow, bruschetta, I can really have some?' Why, yes you can, with this gluten-free version. This bruschetta goes particularly well with Potted trout (see page 186).

140g (1 cup) brown rice flour

1½ tablespoons sugar

1¾ teaspoons gluten-free baking powder

½ teaspoon salt

1 egg, lightly beaten

125ml (½ cup) milk or soy milk

2 tablespoons vegetable oil, for brushing

TOMATO SALSA
Makes 250g

250g baby heirloom tomatoes or cherry tomatoes, diced

2 tablespoons chopped basil leaves

1 small red onion, finely chopped

a generous splash of raspberry vinegar

a splash of extra virgin olive oil

Preheat the oven to 180°C. Grease and line six mini loaf tins (6.5 x 10cm). Line a baking tray with baking paper.

Combine the flour, sugar, baking powder and salt in a large bowl. Beat the egg, milk and oil in a separate bowl.

Add the wet ingredients to the dry ingredients and mix to combine well. Pour into loaf tins. Bake for 15–20 minutes, until a skewer inserted into the middle comes out clean. Remove from the oven and set aside to cool.

Slice each loaf lengthways and brush the cut side with oil. Place on the prepared tray and bake for 5 minutes until golden. Remove from oven to cool. Top with tomato salsa.

To make the tomato salsa, combine the tomato, basil and onion in a bowl and toss well. Add the vinegar and season with salt and pepper.

Place a generous tablespoonful of salsa on each bruschetta slice and drizzle with the oil.

Keep the bruschetta stored in an airtight container in the pantry for everyday use: to nibble on, as bread for lunch or to break up and add to a salad.

POTTED TROUT

Serves 10

This one really is the little entertainer. Make it and keep it in the fridge for a couple of days. It's also great for a picnic or to take to someone's house when they ask for a nibbly to be brought. Serve with Bruschetta (see page 184).

50g butter

2 French shallots, finely diced

a small handful each of chervil and tarragon leaves

250g smoked trout

zest and juice of ½ lemon

50g ghee (clarified butter)

10–12 black peppercorns

a few chervil leaves, for garnishing

Melt the butter in a small frying pan, add the shallot and sweat until opaque. Do not brown. Remove from the heat and stir in the herbs.

Place the trout and lemon zest and juice in a food processor, season with pepper (the trout is salty, so don't add more salt!) and pulse to combine. Add the shallot mixture and pulse again to combine. Spoon into two 250ml (1 cup) ramekins and press flat with a piece of paper towel or the back of a spoon.

Gently melt the ghee in a saucepan, pour over the trout and sprinkle on the peppercorns. Place a chervil leaf, fanned out, next to one of the lonely peppercorns. Set aside to cool and store, covered with plastic wrap, in the fridge.

Party, Party, Party!

This fun collection gives you some great ideas for children's birthday parties, lunchboxes, snacks, afternoon teas and sleepovers. From Princess's Paradise to Ships Ahoy, there's a party theme to suit every occasion and every child. This chapter is for my nieces Phillipa, Eleanor, and Esther, and nephew, Lachlan.

PRINCESS'S PARADISE

The prettiest treats to make any little princess's day perfect.
Eleanor, because we share the same birthday, this one's for you.

STRAWBERRY MOCKTAILS
Makes 4 little tea cups

150g (1 cup) chopped strawberries

125g (½ cup) low-fat natural yoghurt

70g (½ cup) ice cubes

POWDER PUFFS
Makes 12

3 eggs, separated

170g (¾ cup) caster sugar

75g rice flour

100g (¾ cup) gluten-free cornflour

¾ teaspoon cream of tartar

½ teaspoon bicarbonate of soda

½ cup whipped cream

pure icing sugar, sifted, for dusting

Strawberry Mocktails: Place all the ingredients in a blender and puree. Pour into cocktail glasses and serve.

Powder Puffs: Preheat the oven to 200°C. Line two baking trays with baking paper.

Whisk the egg whites in a large bowl with electric beaters until soft peaks form. Gradually add the caster sugar and beat until the meringue mixture is thick and glossy. Add the egg yolks, one at a time, beating well after each addition. Sift in the flours, cream of tartar and bicarbonate of soda and fold in very gently and thoroughly with a large metal spoon until firm (when spooned onto the trays the mixture should not settle or run).

Spoon heaped teaspoons of the mixture onto the prepared trays, allowing room (2cm) for spreading. Bake for 20 minutes, checking every 5 minutes. Allow the cakes to rest on the trays for 1 minute, then, using a spatula, transfer to a wire rack to cool completely. Store in an airtight container for at least 3 hours, then sandwich puffs together with a spoonful of whipped cream in the middle. Dust the puffs with the icing sugar, place on a tiered cake stand and serve.

The puffs, without the filling, can be made a day ahead. There is no need to place them in the fridge overnight, store in a cool section of your pantry in an airtight container. When the puffs are ready to be filled, you can add some shaved chocolate to the cream or use a really thick yoghurt.

PRINCESS'S PARADISE

PRINCESS FRUIT WITH CHOCOLATE

½ watermelon

½ rockmelon

400g dark cooking chocolate, chopped

250g strawberries, hulled

MOUTH-WATERING RASPBERRY ANGEL CAKE

Serves 10

6 eggs, separated

300g (1⅓ cups) caster sugar

juice of ½ lemon

200g potato flour

Princess Fruit: Line a tray with baking paper. Cut the watermelon and rockmelon into 3cm-thick slices. Place the fruit on a work surface and, using shaped cutters, cut into the desired shapes – stars, diamonds, angels, or the number of the birthday girl – maximising the shape with the cutter so you have less wastage. Place the chocolate in a heatproof bowl. Pour boiling water into a small saucepan and place the bowl of chocolate on top. Do not let the bowl touch the water. Stir until the chocolate has melted. Half-dip the fruit shapes and strawberries in the melted chocolate and place onto paddle-pop sticks. Insert the paddle-pop sticks into floral foam and wrap base in a decorative napkin and tie with string.

Angel Cake: Preheat the oven to 180°C. Grease and line a 20cm springform cake tin.

Place the egg yolks, sugar and lemon juice in a large bowl and beat with electric beaters on high for 5–8 minutes, or until pale and thick. Gently mix in the potato flour on low speed for 2 minutes, or until thoroughly combined.

In a separate large bowl, beat the egg whites until stiff peaks form. Fold the egg yolk mixture into the egg whites with a spatula. Pour into the prepared tin and bake for 35–45 minutes, until golden or a skewer inserted into the middle comes out clean. Cool in the tin for 20 minutes, then turn the cake out onto a cake plate or cake stand.

 continued

PRINCESS'S PARADISE

continued

ICING*

375g (3 cups) pure icing sugar, sifted

3 teaspoons softened butter

60ml (¼ cup) milk

200g (½ cup) smashed raspberries

*For dairy-free icing, refer to Delicate feathery sponge recipe (page 104)

To make the icing, combine the sugar, butter, milk and half of the raspberries in a heatproof bowl over a saucepan of simmering water and stir until the icing is soft and spreadable. If the icing is too thick, add a teaspoon of milk. Spread the remaining raspberries over the top of cake with a knife. Pour the icing on top and, using the back of a spoon, gently spread it over the raspberries, moving from the centre to the edge so that the icing dribbles down the edge.

Decorate with candles and serve.

SHIPS AHOY

An excellent spread for a pirate-themed birthday party, kids will enjoy the nautical look of these tasty treats.

JELLY BOATS
Makes 8

4 large oranges

2 x 135g packets of different flavoured jelly, such as raspberry, strawberry, peach, orange or lime

4 sheets of edible rice paper

SAIL FRUIT
Makes 8

1 lemon wedge

4 apples, halved with core removed

24 grapes, seedless

8 slices watermelon, cut into triangles

Jelly Boats: Cut the oranges in half from top to bottom. With a small sharp knife, remove the inside flesh of the oranges and carefully scrape out the membrane taking care not to make a hole in the skin. Place the hollow orange halves in muffin moulds.

Make up the jelly following the packet instructions but using only half the amount of water required (a more concentrated jelly will hold its shape).

Fill each orange half to the top with the jelly and refrigerate for 2 hours until set. Trim the edges of your set jelly oranges with scissors.

Cut out 8 triangles of edible rice paper and thread onto toothpicks to make the sails. Attach the rice paper sails and serve immediately (the jelly boats will start to turn soggy if left for too long).

Sail Fruit: Squeeze some lemon juice over the apple halves so they don't go brown. Stand a paddle-pop stick mast in each apple half. Fill the cavity in the apple with the grapes. Slide a watermelon triangle down a paddle-pop stick mast to form a sail.

SHIPS AHOY

SEA SHANTY FISH PIECES
Serves 6–8

60g (2 cups) gluten-free cornflakes

50g (½ cup) grated Parmesan

1 tablespoon finely chopped flat-leaf parsley

2 egg whites

60g (½ cup) gluten-free cornflour

1kg boneless fish fillets such as ling, cut into 3cm cubes

Preheat the oven to 170°C. Line a baking tray with baking paper.

Place the cornflakes in a plastic bag and seal. Use a rolling pin to coarsely crush the cornflakes.

Tip the crushed cornflakes into a shallow bowl. Add the Parmesan and parsley, season with salt and pepper and stir to combine.

Lightly whisk the egg whites in another shallow bowl. Place the cornflour in a third bowl.

Coat the fish pieces in the cornflour, then dip in the egg white and finally roll in the cornflake crumbs. Transfer to the prepared tray and spray with olive oil cooking spray. Bake for 10 minutes, then turn and bake for a further 10 minutes until golden. Remove from the oven.

If you like, curl paper bags into cone shapes and divide the fish pieces between the paper cones. Wrap the base of each cone with a small paper napkin, place on a platter and serve.

SHIPS AHOY

CHOCOLATE GANACHE BOAT

Serves 12

225g (2½ cups) desiccated coconut

30g (½ cup) shredded coconut

230g (1 cup) caster sugar

4 egg whites, lightly beaten

375ml (1½ cups) rice milk, chilled

750g dark chocolate bits

Preheat the oven to 170°C. Lightly grease and line a 22cm oval springform cake tin.

Combine the coconuts and sugar in a large bowl. Make a well in the centre and add the egg whites. Combine well with your hands.

Firmly press the coconut mixture into the base and around the sides of the prepared cake tin to form a tart shell approximately 2cm thick. Line with baking paper and pastry weights or uncooked rice and blind bake for 30 minutes, or until golden and crispy to touch. Remove from the oven, place the tin on a wire rack and allow the tart shell to cool completely.

To prepare the chocolate ganache, pour the rice milk into a non-stick saucepan over low heat and add one-third of the chocolate. Stir continuously until the chocolate melts. Add half of the remaining chocolate and continue to stir until melted. Add the remaining chocolate and stir until smooth and melted. Do not leave the saucepan unattended over the heat or your sauce will go lumpy. Set aside to cool and thicken for 5 minutes.

Remove the coconut tart shell from the tin and transfer to a serving plate or board.

Pour the chocolate ganache into a jug and pour into the coconut tart shell until 1cm from the top. Carefully place in the refrigerator overnight to set.

Decorate the top of the cake with mini sailing boats in a circular pattern or in the shape of the age of the birthday boy or girl, or make a heart sail as we did. Cut with a hot sharp knife, into square pieces approximately 3cm wide.

HAPPY LITTLE PEOPLE

Little people make me smile. They give me so much happiness with their smiles and comments about their day. I remember chopping strawberries for a pavlova once and before the berries could even hit the dessert my niece Esther had devoured the whole punnet – she loves them. It's important that children fall in love with fruit and flavour – and fewer sweeties.

FRUIT KITE
Makes 1

1 watermelon triangle

1 rockmelon triangle

10 blueberries

2 small pineapple wedges

CHOCOLATE JUNGLE FRUIT
Makes 24

4 kiwi fruit, peeled and sliced

4 bananas, peeled and cut into thirds

500g milk, dark or white chocolate, chopped

Fruit Kite: Arrange the triangles of watermelon and rockmelon in the shape of a kite on a plate.

Thread the blueberries onto a piece of string to make the tail of the kite with a darning needle, then thread the pieces on the plate onto the string in the shape of a kite, adding a pineapple wedge at each end to create bows. Make a knot at both ends. You will probably want to make several kites to place on the party table, depending on how many children are attending.

Jungle Fruit: Line a tray with baking paper. Have ready 24 paddle-pop sticks and one piece of 15 x 15cm floral foam.

Slide each piece of fruit onto one end of a paddle-pop stick and set aside. Place the chocolate in a heatproof bowl. Pour boiling water into a small saucepan and place the bowl of chocolate on top. Do not let the bowl touch the water. Stir until the chocolate has melted.

Dip the fruit into the chocolate and place flat on the prepared tray. Refrigerate for 5 minutes.

Remove the fruit from the fridge and, if you like, insert the paddle-pop sticks into floral foam in rows of four or serve on a plate.

HAPPY LITTLE PEOPLE

ICE-CREAM DAISIES
Makes 6

500g dairy-free ice-cream or sorbet (we used banana and mango sorbet adapted from the recipe on page 142)

6 large white marshmallows

3 thin strips of liquorice, halved

black icing writing, for decorating

MONKEY JUICE
Serves 4 in little people cups (50ml each)

115g (½ cup) mashed ripe banana

125ml (½ cup) skim milk or rice milk

125g (½ cup) low-fat natural yoghurt or soy yoghurt

100g (¾ cup) ice cubes

1 teaspoon honey

Ice-cream Daisies: Spoon one scoop of ice-cream or sorbet into six 80ml (⅓ cup) ice-cream containers. Place in the freezer for 30 minutes.

Meanwhile, cut the large marshmallows into fours. Remove the ice-cream containers from the freezer and place a scoopful in each of the 6 patty cases. Place your marshmallows like a daisy on top. Curl a thin piece of licorice and place at the centre of each daisy.

Return to the freezer for 30 minutes or overnight. Serve straight from the freezer.

Monkey Juice: Combine all the ingredients in a blender and mix or pulse for 2 minutes. Pour into party cups and serve.

HAPPY LITTLE PEOPLE

FAIRY CAKES
Makes 24

125g butter, softened

170g (¾ cup) caster sugar

140g (1 cup) potato flour

175g (1 cup) rice flour

2 tablespoons gluten-free baking powder

185ml (¾ cup) milk

2 eggs, lightly beaten

1 teaspoon vanilla extract

125ml (½ cup) cream

1–2 drops of pink or blue food colouring or 1 teaspoon blueberry or strawberry jam

pure icing sugar, sifted, for dusting

Preheat the oven to 180°C. Line two 12-hole 80ml (⅓ cup) muffin tins with paper cases.

Place the butter, sugar, flours, baking powder, milk, eggs and vanilla in a bowl and beat on high speed with electric beaters for 3 minutes, until pale and smooth like a batter. Spoon the mixture into the paper cases and bake for 10–15 minutes, until golden brown or when a skewer inserted into the middle comes out clean. Leave to cool in the tray for 5 minutes then turn out onto a wire rack to cool completely.

Cut a 3cm circle out of the top of each cake, then cut in half to create two semicircles for the wings. Whip the cream in a small bowl until soft peaks form, then beat in the colouring or jam. Spoon the cream onto the cakes, arrange the wings on top and dust with the icing sugar.

NOT-SO-SLEEPY SLUMBER PARTY

The eldest of four girls, I remember my first slumber party. So do my parents! They came down from their slumber to keep us quiet several times. We talked, laughed, and ate our way through the night and were thoroughly exhausted the next day – it was so much fun! Here's some funky food with sustenance for a very long evening of nattering.

NOT-SO-NUTTY ROCKY ROAD
Makes 18–20 pieces

180g (2 cups) marshmallows, roughly chopped

30g (1 cup) puffed rice

70g (½ cup) hazelnuts, toasted and roughly chopped

50g sultanas

50g fresh or frozen raspberries or cranberries

375g dark chocolate, chopped

HONEY POPCORN
Serves 6-8

115g (⅓ cup) honey

60g butter

95g (½ cup, lightly packed) brown sugar

½ tablespoon milk

50g (4 cups) popped popcorn

Rocky Road: Line a tray with baking paper.

Combine the marshmallows, puffed rice, hazelnuts, sultanas and raspberries or cranberries in a large bowl.

Place the chocolate in a heatproof bowl over a saucepan of simmering water. Do not let the bowl touch the water. Stir until the chocolate is melted and smooth.

Pour the chocolate onto the marshmallow mixture and stir until well combined. Spoon onto the prepared tray and allow to set. Break into random pieces and serve.

You can prepare this rocky road a day or so ahead and store the pieces in an airtight container.

Honey Popcorn: Preheat the oven to 180°C. Line a baking tray with baking paper.

Heat the honey, butter, brown sugar and milk in a saucepan over low heat and stir until smooth. Take off the heat, add the popcorn and stir to combine. Spread onto the prepared tray and bake for 10 minutes, or until crisp and golden. Watch carefully to make sure the popcorn doesn't burn.

Serve in a large bowl for all to share or in individual containers.

NOT-SO-SLEEPY SLUMBER PARTY

BERRY AND CHOCOLATE TRIFLE CAKE (EGG-FREE)

Serves 8

390g (3 cups) quinoa flour

85g (⅔ cup) gluten-free cocoa powder

2 teaspoons gluten-free baking powder

460g (2 cups) caster sugar

250ml (1 cup) vegetable oil

1 tablespoon vanilla extract

500ml (2 cups) water

2 tablespoons white vinegar

500g fresh or frozen raspberries

200g grated dark chocolate, shaved

300ml thickened cream or soy cream, whipped

BERRY SMOOTH SMOOTHIES (DAIRY-FREE)

Serves 2

150g (1 cup) mixed berries

125g (½ cup) natural soy yoghurt

70g (½ cup) ice cubes

2 teaspoons honey

Trifle: Preheat the oven to 180°C. Lightly grease and line two 20cm springform cake tins.

Mix the flour, cocoa, baking powder and sugar in a large bowl and make a well in the centre.

Combine the oil, vanilla and water in a separate bowl.

Pour the wet ingredients into the dry ingredients and stir until smooth. Add the vinegar and quickly mix well. Immediately divide the mixture between the two prepared tins.

Scatter 100g of the berries over the top of the two cakes and bake for 25–30 minutes, or until firm and springy. Remove from the oven and cool in tins on a wire rack.

Turn out onto a chopping board and cut each cake into quarters. Place three quarters in the base of a medium-size serving bowl. Sprinkle on one-quarter of the shaved chocolate, spoon one-third of the cream on top, then scatter on one-third of the remaining raspberries. Repeat the layering process two more times, finishing with a layer of chocolate. Cover with plastic wrap and refrigerate until ready to serve. Serve in individual bowls or one very large bowl and enough spoons for your all your guests.

Smoothies: Combine all the ingredients in a blender and process on high speed for 1 minute. Serve with thick-tubed straws.

The Science of Flours

Gluten-free baking and cooking is not only an art but a science. This section contains information and tips on the many different flours I have experimented with over the years in my quest to get the best possible flavour and texture.

THE SCIENCE OF FLOURS

Most of the flours listed below are available in the health food aisle of the supermarket or from health food stores. Always use a gluten-free flour from the recipe to dust surfaces before kneading dough.

Get in touch, literally, with your flours. Take a third of a cup of the flour and feel it. Rub it between your thumb and forefinger. Is it squeaky? Is it soft and powdery or is it gritty and earthy? If you add a little water does it stick together and expand or does it separate? Channel your inner professor and become a curious cook – once you get to know how different flours work, you'll soon be making breads, pastries, pies and tarts from scratch.

For me, baking is a labour of love and a simple thing like bringing a tart or cake to the table makes all the time given to that quiet science worthwhile.

Amaranth flour (6) is made from the seed of the amaranth plant, a leafy vegetable, and has a beautiful, earthy taste. Perfect for pizza dough and savoury pie pastry. Puffed amaranth, similar to puffed rice, makes for a yummy porridge and is a great protein boost first thing in the morning.

Arrowroot flour (1) is a fine powder ground from the root of the plant. It is tasteless and turns clear when cooked which makes it ideal for thickening clear sauces and getting a group of flours to work well together – use in anything that requires a little 'glue'. Only add this flour to cold or lukewarm ingredients and gradually increase the heat while stirring frequently (adding directly to hot ingredients will cause it to separate).

Brown rice flour (10) is milled from unpolished brown rice. It is heavier than white rice flour and has a higher nutritional value. It also has higher fibre content as it contains bran. Great for biscuits, sweet and savoury breads, and pancakes.

Buckwheat flour (12) is not, despite its name, a form of wheat and is actually made from the seed of a plant that is related to rhubarb. It has a strong nutty taste and is not generally used on its own, but blended with rice flour or gluten-free cornflour to weaken the flavour. Perfect for savoury pastry, muffins and banana bread.

Polenta flour (3), sometimes called cornmeal or maize flour, is used in countries all around the world. It has a gelatinous texture when cooked that increases the heartiness of a meal – during the potato famine it was relied upon as a staple food. It is a coarse grain and very absorbent so it can be moulded into shapes and turns crunchy when made into fritters. Once thought of as peasant food it is now popular in many a fine-dining establishment. **Fine polenta** (8) is less coarse than regular polenta and turns soupy when mixed with water. Fantastic for use in bread, scones, bikkies and all sorts of baking.

Potato flour (4), not to be confused with potato starch flour, is a heavy flour with a strong potato flavour so a little goes a long, long way. Add to casseroles for thickening as you would with cornflour and use in pastries for crispness. Only add this flour to cold or lukewarm ingredients and gradually increase the heat while stirring frequently (adding directly to hot ingredients will cause it to separate).

Potato starch flour (11) is a fine white flour made from potatoes with a light potato flavour that is undetectable when cooked. Perfect for sponge cakes and shortbread. Only add this flour to cold or lukewarm ingredients and gradually increase the heat while stirring frequently (adding directly to hot ingredients will cause it to separate).

Quinoa flour (9) (pronounced 'keen-wah') is made from a plant related to spinach and beets and although commonly considered a grain is actually a seed. It has been used for over 5,000 years as a cereal and is a good source of vegetable protein. This flour bakes beautifully in cakes and pastries, and quinoa puffs are an excellent replacement for couscous and make a honey-tasting porridge.

Rice flour (5), available from Asian supermarkets, is a fine-grade white rice flour and has a more delicate cooked texture. Chinese rice flour is made from long-grain rice, whereas Japanese rice flour is milled from Japonica or calrose short-grain rice. Use in noodles, pastry, sponge cakes and bread. Only add this flour to cold or lukewarm ingredients and gradually increase the heat while stirring frequently (adding directly to hot ingredients will cause it to separate).

Soy flour (7) is high in protein with a nutty taste. It's not generally used on its own in recipes as the taste can be overwhelming, but works well when combined with other flours. It has a higher fat content which make it a great substitute for eggs in cakes and pastries when mixed with other flours and water.

Tapioca flour (2) is made from the root of the cassava plant. It adds chewiness to baked dishes and is a good thickener. Use in casseroles, meat or vegetables patties. Only add this flour to cold or lukewarm ingredients and gradually increase the heat while stirring frequently (adding directly to hot ingredients will cause it to separate).

INDEX

A

almond, rosewater and cherry cakes 118
apples
    apple and berry miniettes 166
    apple, leek and pumpkin gratin 54
    tarte tatin 140

B

banana upside-down puddings 172
basil with pine nuts and garlic pasta sauce 96
beef
    beef Wellington 58
    burgerettes 42
beet and orange salad 38
berries
    berry and apple miniettes 166
    berry and chocolate buckwheat hotcakes 12
    berry and chocolate trifle cake (egg-free) 204
    berry ricotta cake 112
    berry smooth smoothies (dairy-free) 204
biscotti, pistachio 164
biscuits
    delicate lavender shortbread 160
    gooey dark choc and orange biscuits 152
    lemon and ginger biscuits 158
    melting moments 148
    pistachio biscotti 164
blueberry, maple and mascarpone tart 132
bread
    bruschetta 184
    burgerettes 42
    chia bread 24
    chicken sandwiches 40
    coconut and cinnamon bread 14
    herbie flatbread 178
    rice flour buns 44
breadcrumbs 80
bruschetta 184
buns, rice flour 44
burgerettes 42

C

cakes
    almond, rosewater and cherry cakes 118
    berry and chocolate trifle cake (egg-free) 204
    berry ricotta cake 112
    chocolate ganache boat 197
    cocoa sponge cakes 114
    decadent chocolate mousse cake 102
    delicate feathery sponge 104
    fairy cakes 201
    layered meringue cake with seasonal fruit 134
    lemon and ricotta cheesecake 126
    lemon and saffron teacake 108
    lime and coconut island cake 110
    mouth-watering raspberry angel cake 192
    orange and cardamom syrup cake 106
    polenta heart cakes 116
    strawberry shortcakes 120
cheese
    mint, goat's cheese and chutney miniettes 168
    stuffed dates 180
    tomato, onion and goat's cheese tart 72
cheesecake, lemon and ricotta 126
cherry, almond and rosewater cakes 118
chia bread 24
chicken
    chicken sandwiches 40
    chicken schnitzel 50
    chicken soup pies 80
    roast chook with lemon, thyme and Szechuan salt and pepper 48
chocolate
    berry and chocolate buckwheat hotcakes 12
    berry and chocolate trifle cake (egg-free) 204
    chocolate ganache boat 197
    chocolate jungle fruit 198
    chocolate pavlova 138
    chocolate soufflés 122
    cocoa sponge cakes 114
    decadent chocolate mousse cake 102
    gooey dark choc and orange biscuits 152
    princess fruit with chocolate 192
chutney, my favourite 169
cocoa sponge cakes 114
coconut
    coconut and cinnamon bread 14
    lemon and coconut macaroons 154
    lime and coconut island cake 110
coleslaw, sweet and spicy 34

D

dates, stuffed 180
decadent chocolate mousse cake 102
delicate feathery sponge 104
drinks
    berry smooth smoothies (dairy-free) 204
    monkey juice 200
    strawberry mocktails 190

E

eggs
- quiche à la rowie 82
- friendly frittata 30

F

fairy cakes 201
fish and seafood
- friendly frittata 30
- paella 64
- potted trout 186
- sea shanty fish pieces 196
- whole baked salmon with smashed peas, lemon and chervil 66

flatbread, herbie 178
frittata, friendly 30
fruit
- chocolate jungle fruit 198
- fruit kite 198
- hot and cold fruit salad 20
- princess fruit with chocolate 192
- sail fruit 194

G

gnocchi with sage and pine nuts 98
goat's cheese, mint and chutney miniettes 168
gooey dark choc and orange biscuits 152
gratin, apple, leek and pumpkin 54

H

herbie flatbread 178
honey popcorn 202
hot and cold fruit salad 20
hotcakes, berry and chocolate buckwheat 12

I

ice-cream daisies 200

J

jelly boats 194

L

lamb, roast, with cider vinegar 62
lasagne 92
lavender shortbread 160
layered meringue cake with seasonal fruit 134
lemon
- classic lemon tarts 130
- lemon and coconut macaroons 154
- lemon and ginger biscuits 158
- lemon and ricotta cheesecake 126
- lemon and saffron teacake 108
- lemon meringue pie 144
- lemon, olive oil and macadamia pasta sauce 96

lime and coconut island cake 110

M

macaroons, lemon and coconut 154
maple slice 150
marscapone, blueberry and maple tart 132
melting moments 148
meringue cake with seasonal fruit 134
meringue pie, lemon 144
miniettes, apple and berry 166
miniettes, mint, goat's cheese and chutney 168
mocktails, strawberry 190
monkey juice 200
morning slice 162
mousse cake, decadent chocolate 102
mouth-watering raspberry angel cake 192
muffins
- apple and berry 166
- mint, goat's cheese and chutney 168

muesli, toasted 22
mushroom and basil stuffed baked onions 56
mushrooms and pumpkin in very flaky pastry 76

N

nectarine tart 128
not-so-nutty rocky road 202
nuts, toffeed 182

O

onions, mushroom and basil stuffed 56
onion, tomato, and goat's cheese tart 72
oranges
- baby beet and orange salad 38
- gooey dark choc and orange biscuits 152
- orange and cardamom syrup cake 106

P

paella 64
parsley and quinoa salad 36
passata, tomato 96
pasta
- fresh pasta 90
- lasagne 92

pasta sauces 96
pavlova, chocolate 138
pie, lemon meringue 144
pies, chicken soup 80
pistachio biscotti 164
pizza, traditional 88
poached stone fruit 18
polenta heart cakes 116
popcorn, honey 202
pork belly with prunes and quinoa 60
potato gnocchi with sage and pine nuts 98
potted trout 186
powder puffs 190
princess fruit with chocolate 192

puddings
    banana upside-down puddings 172
    rice pudding with poached stone fruit 16
    spiced one-cup puddings 170
pumpkin, apple and leek gratin 54
pumpkin and mushrooms in very flaky pastry 76

Q
quiche à la Rowie 82
quinoa and parsley salad 36

R
raspberry angel cake 192
rhubarb strawberry layer wafers 156
rice
    paella 64
    rice pudding with poached stone fruit 16
    saffron rice with pistachio and radish 32
ricotta berry cake 112
ricotta and lemon cheesecake 126
risoni, vegetable 68
roast chook with lemon, thyme and Szechuan salt and pepper 48
roast lamb with cider vinegar 62
rocky road 202

S
saffron rice with pistachio and radish 32
sail fruit 194
salads
    baby beet and orange salad 38
    hot and cold fruit salad 20
    parsley and quinoa salad 36
    sweet and spicy coleslaw 34
salmon
    friendly frittata 30
    whole baked salmon with smashed peas, lemon and chervil 66
sandwiches, chicken 40
sandwiches, sushi 28
sauces
    basil with pine nuts and garlic 96
    béchamel 94
    lemon, olive oil and macadamia 96
    my favourite chutney 169
    tomato passata 96
sausage rolls, homemade 84
schnitzel, chicken 50
sea shanty fish pieces 196
seafood *see* fish and seafood
shortbread, delicate lavender 160
slice, maple 150
slice, morning 162
smoothies, berry smooth (dairy-free) 204
sorbet sandwiched in melting pastry 142

sorbet, strawberry 142
soufflés, chocolate 122
spiced one-cup puddings 170
sponge, delicate feathery 104
stone fruit, poached 18
strawberries
    strawberry mocktails 190
    strawberry rhubarb layer wafers 156
    strawberry shortcakes 120
    strawberry sorbet 142
stuffed dates 180
stuffing 60
sushi sandwiches 28
sweet and spicy coleslaw 34

T
tarte tatin 140
tartlets 176
tarts (savoury)
    mushrooms and pumpkin in very flaky pastry 76
    tartlets 176
    tomato, onion and goat's cheese tart 72
tarts (sweet)
    blueberry, maple and mascarpone tart 132
    classic lemon tarts 130
    nectarine tart 128
    tarte tatin 140
    tartlets 176
teacake, lemon and saffron 108
toffeed nuts 182
tomato, onion and goat's cheese tart 72
tomato passata 96
trout, potted 186
turkey breast with herb and almond butter 52

V
vegetable lasagne 92
vegetable risoni 68

W
wafers 156

HarperCollinsPublishers

First published in Australia in 2011
by HarperCollins*Publishers* Australia Pty Limited
ABN 36 009 913 517
harpercollins.com.au

Copyright © Rowie Dillon 2011

The right of Rowie Dillon to be identified as the author of this work
has been asserted by her under the *Copyright Amendment
(Moral Rights Act) 2000*.

This work is copyright. Apart from any use as permitted under the
Copyright Act 1968, no part may be reproduced, copied, scanned,
stored in a retrieval system, recorded, or transmitted, in any form
or by any means, without the prior written permission of the publisher.

HarperCollinsPublishers
Level 13, 201 Elizabeth Street, Sydney NSW 2000, Australia
31 View Road, Glenfield, Auckland 0627, New Zealand
A 53, Sector 57, Noida, UP, India
77–85 Fulham Palace Road, London W6 8JB, United Kingdom
2 Bloor Street East, 20th floor, Toronto, Ontario M4W 1A8, Canada
10 East 53rd Street, New York NY 10022, USA

National Library of Australia Cataloguing-in-Publication entry:
Dillon, Rowie
Indulge / Rowie Dillon.
978 0 7322 9281 2 (pbk.)
Gluten-free diet—Recipes. Cooking.
Includes index.
641.56318

Cover and internal design by Jane Waterhouse, HarperCollins Design Studio
Cover image and internal photography by Ben Dearnley

Colour reproduction by Graphic Print Group, South Australia
Printed and bound in China at RRD on 157gsm matt art

All spoon measures are level unless otherwise stated
and 1 tablespoon equals 20ml. Cooking temperatures and
times relate to fan-forced ovens. If you are using a
conventional oven, increase the stated oven
temperature by 20°C.

5 4 3 2 1   11 12 13 14 15

ACKNOWLEDGMENTS

A big thank you to Sandy for believing in me. To Helen, Jane, Katherine and Roz from HarperCollins, thank you. To Lalita, Ben, Annalisa and Abigail, lots of love and thanks. Also to Valli and Rebecca, Kevin, Marjorie, Nadine, Steve and Serena, thanks for giving me a break and an opportunity.

To all my family, especially Kylie, Jodie, Simone, Dad, Terrence, Noel and Geoff, Leah, Robert, Alexandra, Nicholas, Jono, Natalie and Dave, and Aunty Mandy and all my nieces and my nephew, I love you and thank you. To my gorgeous friends and mentors who have eaten their way through this piece of work and listened and eaten their way through the growth of my business, an eternal thank you.

A big thank you also to my wholesale clientele, my past and present staff and to all my suppliers; you have all shown so much faith in my creativity and ability. I sincerely thank my customers for their gratitude as it contributes to the fullness in my life and turns what I have into enough and more. It's what makes me thrive and makes every day brighter and lighter.

Thank you also to the following for their generosity, help and support in the creation of this book: The gorgeous Georgie at Major & Tom, Vicki at China Squirrel, Prop Stop, Yolanda and the team from the Natural Food Market, Samantha Robinson, The Bay Tree, Bison Homewares, Accoutrement, Mud Australia, Ginger & Smart, Waterford Wedgewood, Kitchenaid and the team at Peter McGuiness, Food Hardware Bakery Service, Reverse Garbage, Koko Embroidery, Abigail Ulgiati for her grandmother's beautiful cake stand, The Emergency Button, Murdoch Produce, Harris Farm Market, Fine Fish, Lisa & Chris Marinelli for their patience, Cindy & Tony Hearder for their bricks, The Coeliac Society of Australia, Matthew Johnston, Simon and Ariella Perry for allowing Annalisa to work with me on the weekends, Kayleen Flanigan for always being awesome, Celeste Wilde, the wonderful teams at Qantas, Woolworths, David Jones and Thomas Dux Stores, and my little friends Audrey, Edward, Gracie, Olivia and Scarlett.